NATIVE NORTH AMERICAN CHRONOLOGY

Native North American Chronology

Duane Champagne and Michael A. Paré, *Editors*

An Imprint of Gale Research Inc.

I(T)P™

New York • London • Bonn • Boston • Detroit • Madrid
Melbourne • Mexico City • Paris • Singapore • Tokyo
Toronto • Washington • Albany NY • Belmont CA • Cincinnati OH

 NATIVE NORTH AMERICAN CHRONOLOGY

Duane Champagne and Michael A. Paré, *Editors*

Staff

Sonia Benson, *U·X·L Associate Developmental Editor*
Carol DeKane Nagel, *U·X·L Developmental Editor*
Thomas L. Romig, *U·X·L Publisher*

Margaret A. Chamberlain, *Permissions Supervisor (Pictures)*

Mary Kelley, *Production Associate*
Evi Seoud, *Assistant Production Manager*
Mary Beth Trimper, *Production Director*

Mary Krzewinski, *Cover and Page Designer*
Cynthia Baldwin, *Art Director*

The Graphix Group, *Typesetter*

 This book is printed on acid-free paper that meets the minimum requirements of American National Standard for Information Sciences—Permanence Paper for Printed Library Materials, ANSI Z39.48-1984.

ISBN 0-8103-9818-4

Printed in the United States of America

I(T)P™

U·X·L is an imprint of Gale Research Inc., an International Thomson Publishing Company ITP logo is a trademark under license.

CONTENTS

READER'S GUIDE

Native North American Chronology explores significant social, political, economic, cultural, and educational milestones in the history of the Native peoples of the United States and Canada. Arranged by year and then by month and day, the chronology spans from prehistory to modern times. Along with more than 80 illustrations and maps and extensive cross references, the volume contains 24 tribal chronologies and a cumulative subject index.

Related reference sources:

Native North American Almanac features a comprehensive range of historical and current information on the life and culture of the Native peoples of the United States and Canada. Organized into 24 subject chapters, including major culture areas, activism, and religion, the volumes contain more than two hundred black-and-white photographs and maps, a glossary of terms used throughout the text, and a cumulative subject index.

Native North American Biography profiles 112 Native Americans, both living and deceased, prominent in fields ranging from civil rights to athletics, politics to literature, entertainment to science, religion to the military. A black-and-white portrait accompanies each entry, and the volume concludes with an index listing all individuals by field of endeavor.

Native North American Voices presents full or excerpted speeches, sermons, orations, poems, testimony, and other notable spoken works of Native Americans. Each entry is accompanied by an introduction and boxes explaining terms and events to which the speech refers, as well as several pertinent illustrations.

Advisors
Special thanks are due for the invaluable comments and suggestions provided by U·X·L's Native North American books advisors:

Naomi Caldwell-Wood
President, American Indian Library Association

Victoria Gale
Librarian, Lodge Grass High School
Lodge Grass, Montana

Comments and Suggestions

We welcome your comments on *Native North American Chronology* as well as your suggestions for topics to be featured in future editions. Please write: Editors, *Native North American Chronology,* U·X·L, 835 Penobscot Bldg., Detroit, Michigan 48226-4094; call toll-free: 1-800-877-4253; or fax: 313-961-6348.

PICTURE CREDITS

The photographs and illustrations appearing in *Native North American Chronology* were received from the following sources:

Cover: From a painting by Robert Lindneux of the Cherokees' Trail of Tears, **Courtesy Woolaroc Museum, Bartlesville, Oklahoma.**

Courtesy of Duane Champagne: pp. xii, xiii, xiv, xv, 4, 60, 67, 140, 141; ©**1989 by Michael Dorris:** p. xx (top); **National Museum of American Art, Washington, D.C./Art Resource, New York:** pp. xx (bottom), xxvi, 68, 70; **Canapress Photo Service/Shaney Romulainen:** pp. xxiii, 165; **Photograph by Molly Braun, courtesy of Carl Waldman:** pp. 2, 3; **Photograph by Dean R. Snow:** pp. 8, 14, 16; **Ohio Historical Society, OHS4749:** p. 9; **Courtesy of Arizona State Museum; University of Arizona, Gila Pueblo, staff photographer:** p. 11; **Courtesy of Troy Johnson:** p. 12; **Cahokia Mounds State Historical Site.** p. 13; **Courtesy of National Anthropological Archives, Smithsonian Institution. Neg. No. 2267-J:** p. 21; **Courtesy of the Rare Books & Manuscript Division, The New York Public Library, Astor, Lenox, and Tilden Foundation:** p. 24; **Courtesy of the National Archives of Canada, Neg. No. C-36647:** p. 26, **Neg. No. C-403:** p. 47, **Neg. No. 1063-H-1:** p. 54, **Neg. No. C-073663:** p. 63, **Neg. No. 906B:** p. 84, **Neg. No. PA 66815:** p. 104; **Reprinted by permission of the Houghton Library, Harvard University:** p. 30; **Courtesy of the U.S. Department of the Interior and the National Park Service:** p. 34; **Courtesy of the National Archives of Canada:** p. 37; **Courtesy of the American Indian Studies Center, University of California at Los Angeles:** p. 41; **Art Gallery of Ontario:** p. 44; **Photograph by Thane L. Bierwert, courtesy of the Department of Library Services, American Museum of Natural History:** p. 45; **Courtesy of the Glenbow Archives, Cal-**

MAPS OF TRIBAL GROUPS IN UNITED STATES AND CANADA

Federal and state
recognized reservations
in the United States.

Federal Indian Reservations

Federal Indian Reservations

State Indian Reservations

Micmac
Houlton Maliseet
Indian Township
Pennocook
Pleasant Point
Ganienkeh
Penobscot
St. Regis
Nipmuk-Hassanamisko
Abnaki
Oneida
Tonawanda
Onondaga
Tuscarora
Shagticoke
Paugusett
Wampanoag
Oil Springs
Narragansett
Allegheny
Mashantucket
Cattaraugus
Pequot
Paucatuck
Pequot
Shinnecock
Poosepatuck

Bois Forte
Deer Creek
Vermillion Lake
Red Lake
Red Cliff
Devils Lake
Bad River
Grand Portage
White Earth
Leech Lake
L'Anse
Hannahville
Lac Vieux Desert
Bay Mills
Sisseton
Fond du Lac
Sault Ste Marie
Sandy Lake
Ontonagon
Mille Lacs
Grand Traverse
St. Croix
Lac du Flambeau
Sokaogan Chippewa
Crow Creek
Lac Courte-Oreilles
Potawatomi
Upper Sioux
Prairie Island
Oneida
Flandreau
Shakopee
Yankton
Lower Sioux
Menominee
Winnebago
Stockbridge-Munsee
Santee Sioux
Sac and Fox
Potawatomi
Winnebago
Omaha
Isabella
Sac and Fox
Iowa
Kickapoo
Potawatomi
Peoria
Quapaw
Tonkawa
Shawnee
Ottawa
Ponca
Kaw
Wyandot
Otoe
Osage
Seneca Cayuga
E. Shawnee
Miami
Modoc
Cherokee
Creek
Seminole
Choctaw
Iowa
Chickasaw
Shawnee
Potawatomi
Sac and Fox
Kickapoo
Coushatta
Tunica-Biloxi
Alabama Coushatta
Chitimacha

Mattaponi
Pamunkey

Cherokee
Catawba

Mississippi Choctaw

Poarch Creek

Brighton Seminole
Big Cypress Seminole
Dania
Miccosukee

Canadian Native
Culture Groups.

Inuit

Inuit

Inuit

Inuit

Inuit

Inuit

Inuit

Inuit

Inuit

H u d s o n

B a y

Montagnais

Naskapi

Montagnais

Cree

Cree

Montagnais

Cree

Mistassini

Algonkin

Micmac

Cree

Montagnais

Cree

Ojibway

Cree

Micmac

Malecite

Micmac

Ojibway

Abitibi

Ojibway

Micmac

Ojibway

Cree

Ojibway

Algonkin

Algonkin

Mohawk

Abnaki

Ojibway

Ottawa

Mohawk

Ojibway

Cree

Oneida

Ojibway

Delaware

Potawatomi

TRIBAL CHRONOLOGIES

TRIBAL CHRONOLOGIES

For a detailed account of the major events
in the history of these tribal groups, please refer to the index.

Geronimo, Apache warrior
and leader

Apache

A.D. 800 ✦ Arrive in Southwest

1540 ✦ European Contact

Early 1600s ✦ Acquire horses (see pp. 23, 39)

1786-1821 ✦ Spanish-Apache warfare (see p. 25)

1830-50 ✦ Mexican-Apache warfare

1875 ✦ San Carlos Indian Reservation established in Arizona

1878 ✦ Geronimo escapes from San Carlos one year after confinement there (see p. 93)

1880 ✦ Geronimo returns to San Carlos (see p. 93)

1886 ✦ Geronimo imprisoned, then exiled at Fort Sill, Oklahoma, until death in 1909 (see pp. 93, 101)

Cherokee

10,000 B.C. ✦ Arrived in Southeast

A.D. 1539-43 ✦ European contact (see pp. 22, 39-40)

1681 ✦ Cherokee sold as slaves (see pp. 29-30)

1776 ✦ Fight on side of British in Revolutionary War (see p. 52)

1721-1835 ✦ Land cessions (see pp. 54-55, 62)

1821 ✦ Sequoyah creates Cherokee syllabary (see p. 63)

1828 ✦ Cherokee Constitution (see pp. 65, 77)

1838-39 ✦ Trail of Tears (removal) (see pp. 70-73)

1861-65 ✦ Fight for Confederacy in Civil War

1906 ✦ Dissolution of the Cherokee State (see p. 102)

1970s ✦ Tribal government reestablished (see p. 134)

Cheyenne

A.D. 1775 ✦ Migrate to Great Plains and receive Sacred Law (see p. 52)

1850 ✦ Northern and Southern nations divide (see p. 75)

1864 ✦ Sand Creek Massacre (see p. 80)

1866-68 ✦ War for the Bozeman Trail (see p. 81)

1868 ✦ Fort Laramie Treaty (see p. 82)

1876 ✦ Some Northern Cheyenne fight with Sioux at Battle of Little Bighorn (see pp. 86-87)

1877 ✦ Removal to Indian Territory (see p. 94)

1877 ✦ Northern Cheyenne led by Dull Knife and Little Wolf escape Indian Territory (see p. 89)

Early 1880s ✦ Eastern Montana Northern Cheyenne Reservation established (see p. 89)

Dull Knife and Little Wolf, Northern Cheyenne leaders

Chickasaw

A.D. 1540 ✦ European contact (see p. 22)

1801, 1805 ✦ Treaties between the United States and Chickasaw

1813-14 ✦ Fight with General Andrew Jackson against Creek Red Stick warriors (see pp. 61-62)

1828-37 ✦ Land cessions

1838-50 ✦ Chickasaw migrate to Indian Territory (see p. 54)

1856 ✦ Chickasaw Constitution (see p. 77)

1906 ✦ Dissolution of Chickasaw State (see pp. 101-102)

1970s ✦ Tribal government reestablished (see p. 134)

Louise Erdrich, Chippewa
writer

Painting of Choctaw playing ball

Chippewa (Ojibway)

A.D. 1615 ◆ Arrive in Lake Michigan/Lake Superior area (see p. 38)

1660 ◆ Chippewa-Sioux Wars (see p. 38)

1700-1800 ◆ Some Chippewa migrate into Great Plains area (see pp. 38, 51)

1837, 1842, 1854 ◆ Land cessions

1850s ◆ Relocated to reservations (see p. 77)

1889 ◆ Lands alloted (see pp. 94, 97-98)

1980s ◆ Fishing/hunting treaty rights protests (see p. 136)

Choctaw

A.D. 1540 ◆ European contact (see p. 22)

1755 ◆ Choctaw uprising

1801 ◆ First land cession, 2.5 million acres

1831-33 ◆ Removal to Indian territory (see p. 66)

1860 ◆ Choctaw Constitution (see p. 77)

1902 ◆ Lands allotted (see pp. 94, 97-98)

1906 ◆ Dissolution of Choctaw State (see p. 134)

1970s ◆ Tribal government reestablished (see p. 134)

Comanche

A.D. 1300 ◆ Arrive in southern Plains (see p. 46)

1680-1700 ◆ Acquire horses (see p. 50)

1846 ◆ Comanche in Texas come under U.S. control after Mexican-American War (see p. 73)

1870-90 ◆ Peyote religion spreads among Comanche (see p. 84)

1874 ◆ Battle with U.S. forces

1875 ◆ Surrender at Fort Sill

1875 ◆ Assigned to reservation

Creek

10,000 B.C. ◆ Arrive in Southeast

A.D. 1540-42 ◆ European contact (see p. 22)

1812-13 ◆ Red Stick War (see pp. 61-62)

1814 ◆ Battle of Horseshoe Bend (see p. 62)

1820-40 ◆ Removal to Indian Territory (see p. 70)

1867 ◆ Creek Constitution (see p. 77)

1906 ◆ Dissolution of Creek State (see pp. 101-102)

1970s ◆ Tribal government reestablished (see p. 134)

1984 ◆ Poarch Band of Creek federally recognized

Crow

A.D. B.C. 1430 ◆ Arrive on Great Plains (group known as Hidatsa)

1680 ◆ Acquire horses (see p. 50)

1776 ◆ Crow tribe splits from Hidatsa

1840 ◆ Crow establish Sun Dance (see p. 51)

1846-48 ◆ United States takes over Crow lands after the Mexican-American War (see p. 74)

1846-51 ◆ Land cessions

1956 ◆ Proposed $5 million settlement for Crow lands vetoed by President Dwight D. Eisenhower

1981 ◆ State of Montana orders Crow to open access to fishing on Bighorn River

Fox

A.D. 1638-84 ◆ Beaver Wars (see p. 37)

1654 ◆ Move from Michigan to Wisconsin to avoid war with Iroquois (see pp. 32, 37)

1712-18, 1727-37 ◆ War between Fox and French

1804 ◆ Sign Treaty of St. Louis ceding sections of Illinois, Wisconsin, and Missouri for $2,000

Fox chief Chekuskuk and Sauk chief
Keokuk with others

Fox (cont.)

1810 ◆ Begin mining lead in southwestern Wisconsin

1831-32 ◆ Black Hawk War (see pp. 68-69)

1833-40 ◆ Relocated to Indian Territory (see p. 66)

1884-94 ◆ Fox land in Indian Territory opened to U.S.
settlement (see pp. 94-95, 101-102)

Hopi

A.D. 1200-1400 ◆ Hopi emerge from Anasazi culture
(see pp. 10-11)

1150 ◆ Establish the village of Oraibi (see p. 111)

1539 ◆ Spanish contact (see pp. 20-22)

1629 ◆ Spanish missions established among Hopi
(see pp. 34-35)

1680 ◆ Pope's rebellion (see p. 40)

1693 ◆ Spanish reconquest (see p. 40)

1882 ◆ Hopi reservation formed (see p. 91)

1950 ◆ Navajo-Hopi Rehabilitation Act signed (see p. 137)

1974, 1980 ◆ Hopi and Navajo Relocation Act signed
(see p. 137)

Kiowa

A.D. 1430 ◆ Arrive on Great Plains

1680 ◆ Acquire horses (see p. 50)

1846-48 ◆ Fight U.S. Army when it takes control of
Southwest after Mexican-American War (see p. 73)

1867 ◆ Reservation created in Indian Territory (p. 94)

1868 ◆ Fort Laramie Treaty (see p. 82)

1868-1875 ◆ Battles with U.S. forces

1870-90 ◆ Peyote religion spreads among Kiowa (see p. 84)

1875 ◆ Kiowa surrender

1878 ◆ Chief Satanta dies in prison

1903 ◆ *Lone Wolf* v. *Hitchcock* (see p. 100)

Modoc

6,000 B.C. ✦ Arrive in Columbia Plateau

A.D. 1846 ✦ United States takes control of California after Mexican-American War (see p. 74)

1851 ✦ Captain Jack and 50 Modoc warriors hold off an army of 3,000 soldiers for nearly a year (see p. 76)

1869 ✦ Relocated to Klamath Reservation

1870 ✦ Leave reservation

1872-73 ✦ Modoc War

1873 ✦ Surrender and sent to Indian Territory (see p. 94)

1909 ✦ Return to Klamath Reservation

1961 ✦ Federal tribal recognition terminated (see pp. 116, 117)

1986 ✦ Federal tribal recognition restored

Captain Jack, Modoc leader

Mohawk

A.D. 1000-1300 ✦ Arrive in Northeast (see p. 14)

1300-1570 ✦ Cofound Iroquois League (see p. 14)

1534 ✦ European contact (see p. 23)

1676 ✦ Caughnawaga reservation established

1774-84 ✦ Align with British in American Revolution (see pp. 52-53)

1968 ✦ Protest blocks St. Lawrence Seaway International Bridge (see p. 126)

1990 ✦ New York/Canadian confrontation (see pp. 165, 167)

Mohawk standoff

Navajo

A.D. 1200s ✦ Arrive in Southwest

1600-1846 ✦ Navajo raids lead to conflicts with Spanish (see pp. 39, 73-75)

1846 ✦ After Mexican-American War, U.S. takes control of Southwest (see pp. 73-75)

Navajo (cont.)

1862-67 ◆ War between Navajo and U.S. forces
(see pp. 78-79)

1863 ◆ Kit Carson campaigns against Navajo
(see pp. 78-79)

1864 ◆ "The Long Walk," removal to Bosque Redondo
(see pp. 79-80)

1868 ◆ Treaty of Bosque Redondo

1868 ◆ Navajo Reservation created (see pp. 79-80)

1922 ◆ Navajo Tribal Council formed (see p. 112)

1934 ◆ Reject Indian Reorganization Act (IRA)
government (see p. 112)

1941-45 ◆ Serve as "Code Talkers" during World War II
(see pp. 113-114, 154)

1950 ◆ Navajo-Hopi Rehabilitation Act signed into law
(see pp. 91, 137-138)

1959 ◆ Navajo court system established (see p. 118)

1964 ◆ California State Supreme Court upholds right of
Navajo use of peyote cactus in religious ceremonies

1969 ◆ Navajo Community College established
(see p. 125)

Nez Percé

A.D. 1740 ◆ Acquire horses

1805 ◆ Contact with Lewis and Clark expedition
(see p. 59)

1863 ◆ "Thief Treaty" reduces Nez Percé land to one-
tenth its former size (see p. 79)

1873 ◆ Wallowa set aside as Nez Percé Reservation

1875 ◆ Wallowa opened to U.S. settlers

1877 ◆ Nez Percé War (see p. 88)

1877 ◆ Flight of Nez Percé

1877 ◆ Chief Joseph's surrender (see p. 88)

1878 ◆ Consigned to Colville Reservation in Washington

Chief Joseph, Nez Percé
leader

Onondaga

A.D. 1000-1300 ◆ Arrive in Northwest (see p. 14)

1300-1570 ◆ Cofound Iroquois league (see pp. 14, 23)

1649-1700 ◆ Beaver Wars (see p. 37)

1664 ◆ Ally with Dutch and English

1794 ◆ Canandaigua Treaty establishes reservation

1978 ◆ Claim 175,000 acres in New York State

1979 ◆ Win victory for jurisdictional sovereignty

1989 ◆ Twelve wampum belts returned by New York State (see p. 162)

Paiute

A.D. 1776 ◆ European contact

1850s ◆ Arrival of goldseekers (see pp. 72-73, 81)

1869-70 ◆ Wodziwob starts first Ghost Dance movement (see p. 83)

1878 ◆ Relocate to Yakima and Malheur reservations

1890 ◆ Wovoka starts second Ghost Dance movement (see pp. 95-96)

1951 ◆ File claim for $1 billion as Indian share of Comstock Lode silver mine

1957 ◆ Federal tribe recognition terminated (see p. 116, 117)

1980 ◆ Federal tribe recognition restored

Sarah Winnemucca, Paiute interpreter, diplomat, and writer

Pawnee

A.D. 1300 ◆ Arrive in Great Plains

1541 ◆ European contact (see p. 22)

1700 ◆ Acquire horses (see p. 50)

1850s ◆ Attempt to defend hunting territories in Plains against incoming tribes such as Cheyenne and Sioux (see p. 75)

1880s ◆ Extermination of buffalo on the Plains (see p. 90)

Pawnee (cont.)

1874-75 ◆ Removal to Oklahoma Territory
(see pp. 66, 94)

1890s ◆ Adopt Ghost Dancing teachings (see p. 95)

1970-present ◆ Attempt to recover remains of six
Pawnee scouts decapitated in late 1860s
(see pp. 150, 158)

Osceola, Seminole leader

Seminole

A.D. 1750 ◆ Split from Creek, settle in Florida

1817 ◆ Attacked by Andrew Jackson's troops
(see p. 61-62)

1835-42 ◆ Seminole wars (see pp. 62, 70)

1838-41 ◆ Removal to Indian Territory (see p. 66)

1861-65 ◆ Fight for Confederacy in Civil War

1930s ◆ Reservations established in Florida

1970s ◆ Bingo parlor opens

Seneca

A.D. 1000-1300 ◆ Arrive in Northeast (see p. 14)

1300-1570 ◆ Cofound Iroquois league (see p. 14, 23)

1649-1700 ◆ Beaver Wars (see p. 37)

1763 ◆ Pontiac's War (see p. 48)

1799-1815 ◆ Handsome Lake established the Longhouse
Religion (see pp. 58, 133)

1830s ◆ Establish Handsome Lake Church
(see pp. 58, 133)

1830s ◆ Removal to Indian Territory (see p. 66)

1940s-50s ◆ Protest building of Kinzua Dam

1989 ◆ Dispute settlement over taxes levied by state of
New York

Shawnee

A.D. 1675-1700 ◆ Driven out of Cumberland Valley in Southeast by Iroquois, Chickasaw, and Cherokee (see p. 39)

1750s ◆ Form alliance with Delaware to prevent westward colonial expansion (see pp. 48-49)

1768 ◆ Treaty of Fort Stanwix (see pp. 48-49)

1791-95 ◆ Little Turtle's War (see p. 56)

1808-12 ◆ Tecumseh and Tenskwatawa (the Shawnee Prophet) rise to prominence and forge a powerful pan-Indian alliance (see pp. 60-61)

1867 ◆ Cede land in Kansas

1867 ◆ Federal government takes remaining lands

1867 ◆ Relocated to Indian Territory (see pp. 72, 94-95)

Sioux

A.D. 1660-1700s ◆ Many Sioux migrate after Chippewa invade territory in present-day Minnesota (see pp. 38, 51)

1678 ◆ European contact

1862 ◆ Sioux uprising (see p. 79)

1866 ◆ Battle to keep gold miners out of territory (see p. 81)

1868 ◆ Fort Laramie Treaty (see p. 82)

1876 ◆ Battle of Little Bighorn (see pp. 86-87)

1877 ◆ Sitting Bull flees; Crazy Horse surrenders (see pp. 88-89)

1890 ◆ Massacre at Wounded Knee Creek (see pp. 95-97)

1917 ◆ Annuities denied the Minnesota Sioux in 1863 are restored

1954 ◆ Two Sioux tribes displaced by the Oahe and Fort Randall Dam receive more than $10.8 million in compensation

Sitting Bull, Hunkpapa Sioux warrior and leader

Sioux (cont.)

1973 ◆ Three Sioux tribes displaced by the Oahe and Fort Randall Dam receive $14.8 million

1973 ◆ Oglala Sioux and members of American Indian Movement occupy Pine Ridge reservation hamlet of Wounded Knee from February 27 to May 8 (see pp. 138, 142, 145)

1980 ◆ In *U.S.* v. *Sioux Nation*, Sioux win a $122 million judgment for the illegal taking of the Black Hills (see pp. 151-152)

Tlingit

A.D. B.C. 8,000 ◆ Arrive on Northwest Coast

1741 ◆ European contact (see p. 57)

1783 ◆ Fur trade with Russia (see p. 57)

1802 ◆ Drive Russians out of fort at Sitka, Alaska

1804 ◆ Russians retake fort

1806, 1809, 1813 ◆ Tlingit attack Russians

1882 ◆ U.S. Navy shells Tlingit island (see p. 153)

1912 ◆ Alaska Native Brotherhood founded (see p. 103)

1965 ◆ Tlingit win land claims

1970s ◆ Sealaska Corporation formed

1982 ◆ Seek an apology for shelling of Tlingit island (see p. 153)

NATIVE NORTH AMERICAN CHRONOLOGY

11,000 B.C. ◆ **Bering Sea Land Bridge**
Over a period of years small groups of hunters crossed the Bering Sea Land Bridge, also called Beringia, from Asia to Alaska. (The bridge, perhaps 1,000 miles wide at some spots, was formed when lands now under the waters of the Bering Strait were exposed for periods of time.) Eventually these people and their descendants spread throughout North and South America. Over many centuries they slowly moved southward, settling in what are now Canada, the United States, Central and South America, and the Caribbean Islands. *(Also see entry dated 10,000 B.C.: Ice Age ended.)*

11,000 B.C. ◆ **Paleo-Indians**
The Paleo-Indians were the first people to come to the Americas. They lived a nomadic life (having no permanent home and moving from place to place in search of food and water) based on collecting wild plants and hunting animals such as mammoths (very large Ice Age elephants, now extinct), camels, and bison. When food became scarce in one area, the group would move to a new territory, maybe just a few miles away. The leaders of these groups were generally chosen by the tribe for bravery in hunting and war. Most Paleo-Indian groups lived in caves, tents, or shelters that were temporary and could be moved easily to a new area. Hunting and travel were done on foot; horses had disappeared from the continent not long after the first humans arrived. The stone tools of the Paleo-Indian era were used for hunting bison and cleaning the meat. Spear points, axes, scrapers, and knives were skillfully crafted by the Paleo-Indians.

10,200 B.C. ◆ **Family dogs**
Dogs have always been with people in North America. Bones found at several archaeological sites in the western United States show that animals closely related to wolves, but about three-fourths their size, lived with Paleo-Indian people.

HOW DO WE KNOW?

Native North American history dates back thousands of years before there were written documents. There are several ways, however, that we can come to understand aspects of what life was like in North America before the Europeans arrived. Two widely accepted sources of early American history are the science of archaeology—the study of the things previous societies left behind—and the oral traditions that have been passed down from generation to generation among Native American groups.

Archaeologists dig up the ruins of old societies, finding homes and other buildings, as well as tools, arts and crafts, and even foods eaten by ancient cultures. They can date these artifacts through scientific methods. By studying the things people used in their daily lives, archaeologists can make informed judgments about the way people lived in past times.

Most Native American tribes have oral traditions about the past that explain their origins and history. These traditions are made up of a whole network of stories that a group tells about itself. Through these stories a great deal can be learned about the way that group of people perceived the world, and how it has remembered its own history.

Although writing as we know it did not exist in North America before the Europeans arrived, Native peoples had other ways of recording history. Some groups used pictographs, simple pictorial representations of historical events. Pictographs were created on animal hides and on tepees and other dwellings, and were etched into the rocks of cliffs and caves. Other groups used wampum belts, broad woven bead belts, to record treaties and other events.

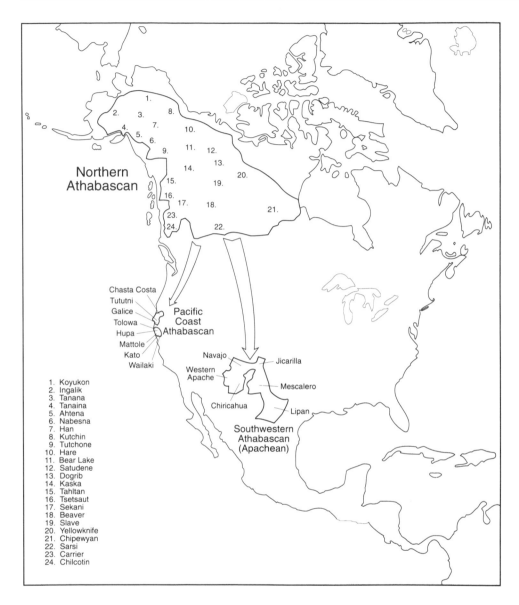

Map of early
Athabaskan
(Athapaskan)
migrations from
the subarctic to
the Southwest
and Pacific
Northwest.

**Northern
Athabascan**

**Pacific
Coast
Athabascan**

Chasta Costa
Tututni
Galice
Tolowa
Hupa
Mattole
Kato
Wailaki

Navajo
Western
Apache
Chiricahua

Jicarilla
Mescalero
Lipan

**Southwestern
Athabascan
(Apachean)**

1. Koyukon
2. Ingalik
3. Tanana
4. Tanaina
5. Ahtena
6. Nabesna
7. Han
8. Kutchin
9. Tutchone
10. Hare
11. Bear Lake
12. Satudene
13. Dogrib
14. Kaska
15. Tahltan
16. Tsetsaut
17. Sekani
18. Beaver
19. Slave
20. Yellowknife
21. Chipewyan
22. Sarsi
23. Carrier
24. Chilcotin

There was less interaction among groups, and cultural differences became clearer. *(Also see entry dated 10,000 B.C.: Ice Age ended.)*

5500 B.C. ◆ Encinitas tradition

A group of cultures emerged in present-day southern California that archaeologists call the Encinitas tradition. These cultures based their economy on coastal resources such as shellfish.

5000 B.C. ◆ Cochise culture

The Cochise culture developed in present-day Arizona and New Mexico. As the environment became mostly arid (dry), the Cochise societies constantly adapted their economic and societal organization to the local conditions. Moving with the change in seasons, the Cochise peoples built homes in cliffs, caves, and desert valleys. By gathering many different plants, the Cochise cultures are believed to have paved the way for the extensive agricultural development in the region by later peoples.

5000 B.C. ◆ Northern Archaic tradition

Hunting and gathering groups, known as the Northern Archaic tradition, began to live in small camps in the Arctic. The hardy groups that inhabited the Arctic hunted caribou, elk, deer, and moose in plains called tundras. These plains in the bitterly cold northern climate consist of a layer of muddy soil covering a permanently frozen subsoil. Only certain plant life, such as moss and some shrubs, can survive in the tundra. The people who lived in this region had to develop very special tools and techniques simply to survive.

CULTURES, SOCIETIES, AND TRADITIONS

Archaeologists use many different terms to describe what they find. As they study ancient Native North Americans they group together information on tribes that have certain things in common. These groups are labeled under the headings of cultures, societies, or traditions. This means that a certain group of tribes that archaeologists define as a culture, society, or tradition lived in a particular era and shared a certain set of beliefs, social habits, and ways of surviving in their environment. The Clovis culture, the Folsom tradition, the Windmiller period, the Adenas culture, and the Hopewell societies are all examples of groupings archaeologists have made of early Native North Americans.

4500 B.C. ◆ Menlo phase

People of the Menlo phase (4500-2500 B.C.) in what is now northern California were the first known groups in North America to build sturdy earth lodges in permanent villages. From these relatively permanent villages the people hunted and collected foods in an area that included mountains and river valleys. In the later part of the Archaic Age (2500 B.C.), however, the climate became more dry, and many groups of the region were forced to leave their homes.

4000 B.C. ◆ Permanent villages in Midwest

Hunters and gatherers of the Archaic Age began building permanent shelters at base camps in what is now southern Illinois. From these camps people would travel throughout the surrounding area to hunt and collect their food.

3000 B.C. ◆ Campbell tradition

In some areas along the coast in southern California, the Campbell tradition replaced the Encinitas tradition. The Campbell tradition was based on hunting deer and other animals as opposed to reaping the coastal food resources, as in the Encinitas tradition. Artifacts (tools and arts and crafts) found from the Campbell tradition included leaf-shaped points and stone mortars and pestles (grinding tools). The people of the Campbell tradition were the ancestors of the modern Chumash of the Santa Barbara area.. *(Also see entry dated 5500 B.C.: Encinitas tradition.)*

3000 B.C. ◆ Early Native American art
The oldest works of art found in North America date back to this time. These are works made on or from stone, bone, antler, and, after 3,000 B.C., ceramics. Earlier Native American art did not survive because it was made of wood, hide, or fibers, which rarely last long in moist soils. Native Americans purposely chose materials that would not last. For most Native peoples, the important thing about an artistic object was its usefulness and its spirit power. They were not at all interested in creating lasting memorials to their skills as artists.

3000 B.C. ◆ Hunting in Alaska
In the Aleutian chain of islands off the coast of Alaska, people skilled at hunting seals, sea lions, and whales built villages with small oval houses, three to five meters (about seven to sixteen feet) in diameter.

3000 B.C. ◆ New foods
With increased trade, maize (a variation of corn initially cultivated in Mexico more than 6,000 years ago), beans, and squash were brought to North America from Mexico. These crops eventually became important food sources.

2600 B.C. ◆ Trade increased
Throughout the Southeast there was an expansion of long-distance trade. Trade helped groups maintain good relations with their neighbors. Methods of using and making tools advanced, because groups that had settled in one region were no longer limited to the resources found within their area. Exotic items such as shells were traded throughout the continent and became important signs of wealth and status.

2500 B.C. ◆ Archaic Age ended
The end of the Archaic Age was marked by the rise of agriculture (farming) in many areas, although not all Indian groups changed from hunting and gathering to agriculture. The growth of agriculture was brought about by the changes in weather conditions and patterns at the end of the Ice Age. The development of agricultural practices had a tremendous effect on the social patterns of many Native American groups. Hunters and gatherers had previously tended to live in small bands that moved frequently and therefore did not form the kind of social and cultural patterns that more settled ways of life brought about. But when care

was taken to plant a crop, a tribe would stay in one place to reap the harvest. As farming methods and tools developed, permanent communities with some form of government often followed. (*Also see entry dated 10,000 B.C.: Ice Age ended.*)

2500 B.C. ✦ Early pottery

Grains and seeds that had been ground into flour or meal required a more leakproof storage system than basketry could provide. Pottery was a major technological advance in the preparation and storage of food and other resources. The earliest pottery north of Mexico was made at sites in present-day Georgia and Florida in 2500 B.C. This pottery was strengthened with plant fibers.

2500 B.C. ✦ Windmiller period

People of the Windmiller period (2500 B.C.-500 B.C.) lived in permanent villages in present-day central California and practiced a wide variety of hunting and gathering activities. They buried their dead in small mounds. The Windmiller people made spearheads out of obsidian (volcanic glass), stone smoking pipes, charmstones, various types of baskets, and grinding stones. The Windmiller peoples were ancestors of the Maidu, Miwok, Ohlone, Winton, and Yokuts.

2000 B.C. ✦ Arctic Small Tool tradition

The Arctic Small Tool tradition developed and spread east as far as Greenland. People in this tradition became the first humans to live in the eastern Arctic, one of the world's harshest environments. These people were the ancestors of the modern Inuit (formerly called Eskimos). They developed remarkable technology—including special harpoons and other techniques for hunting seals, walrus, and whales—which made survival possible.

1500 B.C. ✦ Formative period

The Formative period, also known as the post-Archaic or Classic period, began at this time and lasted until European contact. Despite regional differences, Native American groups during this period had many similarities. Agriculture, ceremonial buildings, trade, village communities, and weaving began to be common among most Native American societies. But throughout North America cultures began to form unique economic, linguistic, political, and religious practices.

1500 B.C. ✦ Northern Archaic tradition

A period of increasing cold pushed the forests in the subarctic towards the south. Northern Archaic tradition hunters, who were adapted to forest environments, also moved south following caribou herds, a major food source. Not long after the Northern Archaic tradition hunters moved south, the area they left was inhabited by Inuit (Eskimo) peoples.

Adena burial
ground in
Miamisburg, Ohio.

1400 B.C. ✦ Mississippi mounds
People who lived along the lower Mississippi River were constructing large burial mounds and living in planned communities. Important people in the tribe
were buried in the mounds, which often had temples built on top of them. The
best-known example of this type of village was Poverty Point, where a massive
semicircle of mounds was constructed. Archaeologists consider these communities the first chiefdoms (villages governed by one principal leader) north of
Mexico.

800 B.C. ✦ Alaskan pottery
The first pottery appeared in Alaska. The style of the pottery and the way it
was made showed that the people in the area may have been in contact with people from Asia.

500 B.C. ✦ Adena culture
The Adena culture developed in the Midwest. The Adena people built burial
mounds and lived in small villages of circular, semipermanent dwellings.

500 B.C. ✦ New pottery and plants
The older practice of using plant fiber to strengthen pottery was replaced in the
Southeast by the use of sand and limestone. A great variety of decorations was
used in pottery-making, showing that different cultures were forming. The new
pottery allowed better storage of foods. People in the Southeast began to grow
native plants like sunflowers, marsh elder, and may grass. The seeds from these
plants were collected and ground to produce flour.

100 B.C. ✦ Hopewell societies

Hopewell societies, interrelated groups centered in present-day Ohio and Illinois, were building massive earthen mounds for burial of their dead and probably for other religious purposes as well. The Hopewell were among the first groups in North America to determine an individual's status in society by the standing of the family he or she was born into, rather than on personal merit. Hopewell societies participated in trade networks that extended from the Great

The Serpent Mound of the Adena or Hopewell culture.

Lakes to the Gulf of Mexico. Some of the items traded were conch shell, shark teeth, mica, lead, copper, and various kinds of stone.

A.D. 1 ✦ Early democracy
In many parts of the East, groups were forming complex social systems. Leaders of these groups often were granted their power by the decision of the group as a whole, by a process similar to modern-day democracy.

A.D. 1 ✦ Hohokam tradition
Small, permanent villages appeared in the Southwest, ending the region's nomadic hunting and gathering lifestyle. In the Sonoran Desert of present-day south-central Arizona, the Hohokam cultural tradition emerged. The Hohokam were hunters and gatherers, but turned to agriculture and developed massive irrigation systems to water their fields. The Hohokam may be ancestors of the present-day Pima and Papago.

100 ✦ Thule or Northern Maritime tradition
All Native North Americans from Alaska to Greenland were part of the same cultural heritage, called the Thule or Northern Maritime tradition. This tradition is recognized for the use of polished slate and elaborately carved bone, and for ivory tools used for hunting sea mammals. The Thule also developed transportation such as dog sleds, kayaks (watertight canoes covered with skins), and umiaks (large open boats made of skins stretched on a wooden frame). These inventions helped the Thule move more quickly and survive in their harsh arctic environment.

200 ✦ Mogollon tradition
In present-day southern New Mexico, eastern Arizona, and parts of Mexico, the Mogollon people developed small villages of earth-covered houses. Later they built multistoried pueblos—small towns made up of stone or adobe (earthen brick) buildings that often housed many families. The Mogollon people developed systems for farming in a dry climate. Some people of the modern Western Pueblos are believed to be descended from the Mogollon.

200 ✦ Patayan tradition
The Patayan tradition covered a vast region in what is now Arizona. The Patayans were among the first pottery producers in the Southwest. Their homes were small and made of wood or stone. They were hunters and farmers, growing squash and corn.

400 ✦ Anasazi tradition
A group called the Anasazi emerged in the Four Corners region of present-day Arizona, New Mexico, Utah, and Colorado. The Anasazi eventually designed

their communities in large multiroomed apartment buildings, some with more than 1,200 rooms! They were farmers. The Anasazi were also skilled potters and were known for the black-on-white geometric designs on their pottery. Modern Pueblo groups of Arizona and New Mexico are descended from the Anasazi.

One of two ball courts found at Snaketown, Arizona. The court is 100 by 130 feet and was built between A.D. 600 and 900.

400 ◆ Bow and arrow
The use of the bow and arrow spread rapidly throughout the continent. This was a major advance in hunting and warfare among many different Native American groups.

450 ◆ Burial mounds
The people of the Lower Mississippi Valley built conical burial mounds and some of the first flat-top mounds in North America. The flat-top mounds were probably built beneath temples or the homes of important people in the village.

500 ◆ Ball courts
A ball game was played in large oval courts in central Arizona. The courts were similar to those found at Mayan Indian ceremonial centers in Mexico.

800 ◆ Toltec site
A group of Mississippian people lived near present-day Little Rock, Arkansas, on what is now called the Toltec site. This site consisted of ten mounds arranged

A series of doorways joining the multistoried rooms and ceremonial chambers of Pueblo Bonito at Chaco Canyon, New Mexico.

around a plaza and enclosed by a two-meter-high (approximately six feet) earth wall. It was the most complex settlement known in the Southeast at the time.

900 ◆ Aztlán

Before European colonization, the area that is now the southwestern United States and northern Mexico was called Aztlán. Aztlán was named by the Aztecs, who built a powerful empire in central Mexico. Many agricultural (farming) communities developed in Aztlán. Southwestern farmers had developed a variety of irrigation systems, such as canals, dams, and various planting methods, to conserve the scarce rainfall in the region. Agriculture had become an advanced and effective food source for the dry region.

Aztlán communities consisted of multistory villages (later named pueblos) and large ceremonial centers. The ceremonial centers resembled *kivas*, the round underground chambers found among the present-day Hopi in Arizona and the Pueblo in eastern New Mexico.

900 ✦ Mississippian period

The cultures of what is now the eastern United States began to transform into the complex societies of the Mississippian period. Farming practices, based on maize and other domestic crops, advanced dramatically within many groups. Many of the Mississippian groups formed elaborate social and political systems. Leadership was hereditary (passed on along family lines) and the villages developed into chiefdoms. The societies participated in long-distance trade and a widespread religion now called the Southeastern Ceremonial Complex, which included elaborate burial customs such as mound building.

950 ✦ Middle Missouri tradition

A group of people migrated to the Great Plains from what are now Minnesota and Iowa, taking with them an advanced knowledge of farming. They settled in present-day South Dakota, where they farmed maize, squash, and other crops that could survive the rough weather. The peoples of the Middle Missouri tradition were the ancestors of the modern-day Mandan and Hidatsa.

985 ✦ First European contact with Inuit

Thule Inuit in Greenland encountered the first expedition of Norsemen (persons from the area now known as Scandinavia) to reach North America.

The Inuit were formerly known as Eskimo, a Cree word rarely used today meaning "raw meat eaters." The Inuit lived in the Canadian Arctic. Inukitut, the Inuit language, was spoken across the entire Canadian Arctic. Population density was low and social groups were usually small. Leadership was generally informal, with no official chiefs. The opinion of the most experienced and respected elder usually carried the greatest weight in group decisions.

All groups relied on hunting land and sea animals, along with fishing. Caribou and seals were the primary food sources, although walrus and whales were hunted by some groups. Because plant life was scarce, gathering played a minor role in the Arctic economy. Delicacies such as berries and birds' eggs were gathered when possible in season.

Caribou (large deer similar to reindeer) were important as food, but also for their hides. The hides were taken in fall when they were in the best condition and used to make winter clothing. For the Inuit, winter clothing consisted of two layers of coats, pants, stockings, and boots; the inner layer of clothing placed the

Great Kiva,
Chetro Ketl
community,
Chaco Canyon,
New Mexico.

fur of the animal hide next to the wearer's skin for warmth. Summer clothing was a single layer and was often made of sealskin. Sealskin boots were also essential for wet conditions. Women's clothing was often more elaborate than men's, with extra space at the back for carrying babies against the mother's skin.

The Inuit lived in large villages in log houses built of driftwood and partly covered by earth. In the winter most groups moved far out onto the sea ice to hunt seal through holes made in the ice. Out on the ice they lived in dome-shaped snow houses, or igloos. These igloos were lighted and heated with lamps made of soapstone; the lamps used whale blubber (fat) as fuel.

1000-1350 ✦ Iroquois Confederacy formed

The Five Nations of the Haudenosaunee, which means "People of the Long-house," consisted of the Mohawk, Oneida, Onondaga, Cayuga, and Seneca. These nations formed a confederation (or association) some time between 1000 and 1350. From that time on, the Five Nations were governed by chiefs from the 49 families who were present at the origin of the confederacy.

Cahokia Mounds, c. 1100-1150. This painting is a reconstruction of the site from across Twin Mounds and Central Plaza to Monk's Mounds.

The Iroquois Confederacy, as it came to be known, began with Deganaw-idah, the Peacemaker, and his spokesperson, Hiawatha. Deganawidah and Hiawatha, trying to stop feuds that had been splitting their people, planted a Great Peace Tree at the Onondaga Nation, near present-day Syracuse, New York. Deganawidah also passed down the Great Law, which was the constitution of the Iroquois Confederacy. The Great Law helped bring peace and unity to the Iroquois people. *(Also see entry dated 1542-1600: Iroquoian peoples.)*

1007 ◆ Leif Eriksson contacted Native Americans

Norwegian explorer Leif Eriksson made one of the first documented European contacts with Native Americans on mainland North America. Inuit, Beothuk, and Micmac peoples encountered him and members of his party along the eastern coast of present-day Canada. *(Also see entry dated 985: First European contact with the Inuit.)*

1040 ◆ Chaco Canyon

Pueblos were flourishing in northern New Mexico's Chaco Canyon. Some pueblos had hundreds of rooms. Among the biggest pueblos were Pueblo Bonito and Chetro Ketl. The pueblos of Chaco Canyon were connected by an extensive road system that stretched many miles across the desert.

1100 ◆ Bad diet

The health of many Mississippian people declined. Their poor health was probably due to overreliance on starchy foods, particularly maize. Beans—a good nutritional complement to maize—did not come into use until A.D. 1300.

Earthen pyramids of Moundville, Alabama.

1100 ✦ Cahokia site

The Mississippian culture had reached its highest level of social complexity. The Mississippian cultural center, now known as the Cahokia site, was near present-day St. Louis, Missouri. There were more than 100 mounds at Cahokia. One of these, Monk's Mound, was the largest ancient construction north of Mexico. Ten thousand people lived in the town surrounding the mounds. *(Also see entry dated 900: Mississippian period.)*

1175 ✦ Awatovi site

Awatovi, in what is now Arizona, was called by the Hopi "Place of the Bow Clan People." Awatovi was thriving in 1175, with about 1,300 ground floor rooms. More than 1,000 people lived there. Later, a two-story pueblo was added. In the sixteenth century, Catholic missionaries built a church at Awatovi.

1300–1600 ✦ Great Temple Mound civilizations

Great Temple Mound or Middle Mississippi civilizations flourished in the river valleys of present-day Alabama, Arkansas, Kentucky, Mississippi, Missouri, Ohio, southern Illinois, southern Indiana, and Tennessee. These societies were organized into republics (societies in which the leader is elected or appointed by the citizens) dominated by a large city surrounded by smaller cities. Each city consisted of a plaza, one or more pyramid-like temple mounds, temples, chiefs' houses, and other houses.

1350 ✦ Moundville

Moundville, in present-day Alabama, was one of the largest ceremonial centers of the Mississippian tradition in the East. It consisted of 20 mounds and a village. Moundville was probably the center of a chiefdom that included several other related communities.

1492 ◆ Columbus arrived in Caribbean

Christopher Columbus and his expedition touched ground on an island in the Bahamas called Guanahani by Natives and San Salvador by Europeans.

1493 ◆ Columbus's second voyage

Columbus undertook his second voyage to the "new world." Returning to San Salvador, Columbus discovered that the Navidad colony he had established had disbanded shortly after his departure. All colonists had been killed by the Taino Indian tribe, who were angered because the Spanish were attacking them. Columbus and his soldiers began a war against the Taino and by 1496 only one third of the native population remained.

EUROPEAN DISEASES DEVASTATED NATIVE AMERICANS

The sixteenth century marked the beginning of a devastating decrease in the Native population of North America. In the next four centuries perhaps as many as 60 million people died, primarily of diseases carried to North America by Europeans. Native Americans had never been exposed to the diseases that were common among the newcomers to their land, such as smallpox, measles, scarlet fever, and influenza (the flu), and therefore had no immunity (natural defenses) to them. With no experience in dealing with these diseases, Native Americans often used ineffective methods in trying to cure the illnesses.

1494 ◆ Taino slavery

Columbus began the enslavement of American Indians, capturing over 500 Taino and sending them to Spain to be sold.

1497–1505 ◆ Vespucci's voyages

Supported by Spain, Amerigo Vespucci explored the West Indies and South America. He is given credit for the discovery of the new world mainland and the American continents are named after him, though whether he even went ashore is not known.

1500s ◆ Horses returned to America

Wild horses (American mustangs) that had escaped from the early Spanish explorers in Mexico came to live on the Great Plains. At that time only a few of the nations that would later make up the High Plains culture were living on the Plains. These peoples lived in small huts and hunted buffalo on foot.

1500 ◆ Columbus established control of San Salvador

Columbus and the people who followed him took control of the Caribbean for Spain. They then began to explore North and Central America. *(Also see entries dated 1492: Columbus arrived in Caribbean; and 1493: Columbus's second voyage.)*

1500 ✦ **Native North Americans in Canada**

The division between Canada and the United States was put in place by Europeans thousands of years after Native North American groups had settled. The history of Canada's aboriginal, or native, people differs in many ways from the history of the Native peoples of the United States. Early Canadian Native groups were smaller than, and not as interconnected as, U.S. groups, and Canada's settlement by European powers did not take the same course as the settlement of the United States. Differences between Native North Americans in Canada and the United States have continued to this day.

1503 ✦ **Trade with European fishermen and whalers**

Various groups along the East Coast began occasional trade with European fishermen and whalers. They frequently exchanged furs and food for metal goods such as iron knives, hatchets, and copper kettles. They also traded for blankets and cloth. European goods soon replaced hand-made objects among the Native peoples.

The Beothuk, who lived on the island now called Newfoundland, were one of the few groups that refused to trade with the Europeans, although they did take some goods from fishermen who dried their fish on land. The Beothuk collected shellfish and hunted both sea and land animals. Bark-covered canoes allowed them to travel out into the stormy north Atlantic to harpoon seals and collect bird's eggs from offshore islands. During the winter the Beothuk hunted caribou.

The Europeans who first contacted the Beothuk gave them the name "Red Indians" because the Beothuk liked to paint their bodies with red ocher (a red-colored clay) and grease. Later the name was applied to other North American Indians, giving rise to the term "Redskins." *(Also see entry dated 1829: Last Beothuk died.)*

1503 ✦ **Jacques Cartier traded with Native Americans**

Near Chaleur Bay, in the Gulf of St. Lawrence along North America's East Coast, Jacques Cartier, a French explorer, traded with a group of Indians. He kidnapped two sons of the Iroquois chief Donnacona. When he took them to France, the youths told stories of the Kingdom of Saguenay, a fictitious kingdom rich in precious metals.

1508-11 ✦ **Destruction of the population of the West Indies**

After Spanish invasions, the Caribbean Indian population was devastated by disease, warfare, and enforced labor. In Puerto Rico the Indian population fell from 200,000 in 1508 to 20,000 in 1511.

1511 ✦ Priests criticized Columbus

Antonio de Montesinos, a Catholic priest, gave a stirring sermon to the Spanish leaders of Hispaniola (the Caribbean island that is now divided between Haiti and the Dominican Republic), condemning them for their treatment of Native Americans. Bartolomé de las Casas, another Spanish priest, wrote *Destruction of the Indies,* in which he described the Spanish conquistadors' (conquering soldiers) cruelty to Native Americans. The priest described the butchering of men, women, and children like "sheep in the slaughterhouse."

1512 ✦ Laws of Burgess

De las Casas and others attempted to stop the cruelty against Native Americans and to change Spanish policies in regard to American Indians. The result of their efforts were the Laws of Burgess, a series of Spanish reforms that outlawed Indian slavery and ordered the owners of *encomiendas*—large amounts of land taken from the Indians—to improve their treatment of Indian laborers.

The Spanish conquistadors could not legally invade, enslave, or take advantage of Native Americans without first reading them the *Requerimiento,* a document outlining the beliefs of the Catholic church. The *Requerimiento* stated that if the Native Americans did not give up their religions and accept the Catholic faith, the Spanish would destroy them.

The *Requerimiento* was supposed to offer Native Americans a chance to surrender peacefully to Spanish rule. But the Spanish ignored both the *Requerimiento* and the Laws of Burgess. Spanish abuses continued against Native Americans for the next four centuries.

1512-21 ✦ Ponce de León and the Fountain of Youth

European belief in mythic waters capable of renewing the old and sick existed before Columbus explored North America. Arawak slaves taken back to Spain by Columbus and other explorers told the Spanish of certain life-giving waters found among Florida's Timucua people. The Spanish took these stories as proof that the Fountain of Youth existed. In 1512 Juan Ponce de León, the governor of Puerto Rico, was given permission by the king of Spain to explore and settle Florida, which the Spanish named *Bimini,* meaning life source. Though one stated goal of Ponce de León's mission was to obtain slaves, it was his search for the fountain for which he was best known. He reached Florida for the first time in 1513 and had extensive contact with the peoples of that region. The Saturiwa and Ai nations opposed his expedition and forced Ponce de León to leave Florida. He returned to Bimini in 1521, but was hit by an arrow. Ponce de León died soon after in Havana (in present-day Cuba) from the wound, never having seen the fabled Fountain of Youth.

1523-24 ◆ Verrazzano explored the Atlantic Coast

Supported by France, Florentine navigator Giovanni da Verrazzano explored the Atlantic coast. Wampanoag, Narragansett, and Delaware Indians encountered the explorer and his party.

1534 ◆ Cartier contacted Micmac

French explorer Jacques Cartier made contact with the Micmac Indians in what is now Canada. The Micmac occupied the present-day areas of the Maritime Provinces, Atlantic Quebec, and southern Newfoundland. They lived near the coast during warm weather. Coastal areas provided fish, shellfish, seabirds and their eggs, and seals. The Micmac used bark-covered canoes for fishing. In winter they moved inland, where they hunted animals such as beaver and moose. To move about on the deep snow of the interior, they used toboggans (a word that came to English from the Micmac). *(Also see entries dated 1535-36: Cartier searched for Saguenay; and 1541-43: Cartier formed settlement in Canada.)*

1535 ◆ De Vaca explored New Mexico

The Spanish explorer Cabeza de Vaca entered present-day New Mexico and reported on the land, food resources, and people.

1535-36 ◆ Cartier searched for Saguenay

Donnacona's two sons, kidnapped by Cartier in 1503, guided the explorer in his search for the Kingdom of Saguenay. The sons led Cartier to their Iroquois village of Stadacona (present-day Quebec City). Cartier continued to sail to Hochelaga (present-day Montreal).

Cartier recorded many details of what he found at Hochelaga. Hochelaga was built well back from the river, beyond extensive fields of corn, for protection against intruders. There, Cartier found about 50 longhouses surrounded by three rows of palisades (fences made of stakes). The palisades had ladders leading up to platforms, where defenders could stand during an attack.

1539-43 ◆ De Soto explored the Southeast

A Spanish expedition led by Hernando de Soto traveled through the present-day southeastern United States. De Soto and his men terrorized the peoples of the area, killing warriors, kidnapping women, and spreading disease. The Spanish found little gold and met strong resistance from the southeastern Indian nations. *(Also see entry dated 1540-1600: Disease destroyed Mississippian culture.)*

1540-42 ◆ Coronado explored Arizona and New Mexico

The Spanish explorer Francisco Coronado traveled into present-day Arizona and New Mexico, and perhaps as far east as present-day Oklahoma. Coronado was

A five-story
Pueblo building.

searching for the Seven Cities of Cíbola, which were believed to contain great
wealth.

There were 98 villages, called pueblos, in present-day New Mexico when the
Spanish arrived. The Pueblo people had similar cultures, but they spoke four distinct languages: Zuni, Keres, Tiwa, and Tewa. Coronado came into contact with
several Pueblo peoples, including the Hopi.

At this time there may have been as many as a dozen Hopi villages along
the Colorado River. Hopi society was divided into 12 groups of clans called
"phratries." Children always belonged to the clan of their mother. Each clan had

French engraving titled "Sauvage Iroquois."

its own sacred objects and ceremonies and each clan shared a version of the same creation story—a story that told how the world and its people came into existence. The Hopi believed that their ancestors originally came to earth from a world below the ground and that the Hopi must honor the spirits in order to be successful. Many Hopi ceremonies sought to create harmony in the community to please the *Kachina* spirits (a group of spirit beings in the Pueblo religions) so they would bring rain to the dry land for Hopi crops.

The populations of the Hopi villages dropped severely because many people died of the diseases brought by Spanish explorers. By 1600 most Hopi had retreated to their present villages in northern Arizona. There the Spanish tried to rule them and spread Christianity, but the Hopi resisted.

1540-1600 ⬩ Disease destroyed Mississippian culture

De Soto and other Spaniards came into contact with people of the Mississippian culture. Diseases brought by the European explorers, fishermen, and slave raiders destroyed the Mississippian culture populations. By 1600 most Mississippian ceremonial centers were abandoned and the surviving people spread throughout the southeastern United States. The structured Mississippian culture, which had been organized around powerful chiefs and priests, gave way and was replaced by egalitarian societies (loosely organized groups in which all members shared the power and responsibility of ruling themselves). These groups are known today as the Caddo, Catawba, Cherokee, Chickasaw, Choctaw, Creek, Natchez, and Pawnee. *(Also see entry dated 1539-43: De Soto explored the Southeast.)*

1541-43 ⬩ Cartier formed settlement in Canada

Jacques Cartier and Sieur de Roberval, the newly commissioned lieutenant-general in Canada, established a settlement near Stadacona. The settlement failed largely as a result of Indian hostility. *(Also see entries dated 1503: Jacques Cartier traded with Native Americans; 1534: Cartier contacted Micmac; and 1535-36: Cartier searched for Saguenay.)*

1542 ◆ **Indians fought from horseback**

The Spanish in Mexico were forced to allow their Indian allies to fight on horseback in order to defeat a serious rebellion. These were the first mounted Indian warriors in the Americas.

1542-1600 ◆ **Iroquoian peoples**

Iroquoian is a word used to describe five New York nations—the Mohawk, Seneca, Cayuga, Onondaga, and Oneida—and other groups who spoke a language similar to the Iroquoians', such as the Huron, the Erie, and the Susquehannock.

The early Iroquois peoples shared a way of life that in many cases was based on intensive farming, fishing, and hunting. Their villages were often palisaded (protected by barriers) because of a history of warfare with other Indian tribes. Iroquoians lived in fairly large communities known for their bark-covered longhouses, which were very long buildings that served as homes, places of worship, and locations for community gatherings. Raised benches or sleeping platforms ran the length of each side, leaving a central area for cooking fires. Fish and corn, as well as personal belongings, hung from the roof of the house or were buried in covered pits.

Iroquoian societies were organized by matrilineal clans—groups of relatives who were related through the mother's side of the family. When Europeans arrived in their territories in the early 1500s, Iroquoian peoples lived along the St. Lawrence River in upper New York state, along the lower Great Lakes, and in the Susquehanna River Valley (in present-day Pennsylvania). *(Also see entry dated 1000-1350: Iroquois Confederacy formed.)*

1565-68 ◆ **St. Augustine established**

The first permanent European settlement in North America was established at St. Augustine, in present-day Florida. The Spanish also established small posts along the Atlantic coastline to present-day Georgia. This area was called Guale.

1568 ◆ **Jesuit Indian school organized**

Jesuits (a Catholic religious order) organized a school in Havana, Cuba, for Indian children brought from Florida, thus establishing the first missionary school for North American Indians. The Spanish wanted to convert the Indians to Catholicism, so Jesuit and Franciscan missionaries taught Native children mainly about religion. *(Also see entry dated 1632: Jesuits began missionary efforts.)*

1579 ◆ **An example of the meeting of two cultures**

Many times the first contact between Europeans and Native Americans resulted in misunderstandings based on a lack of knowledge about each other. When, for example, English explorer Francis Drake anchored off the California coast, he

In 1562, French ships met with Indians near present-day St. Augustine, Florida.

and his crew came upon an Indian tribe known as the Coast Miwok. Drake reported that these people behaved in very strange ways that the sailors could not understand.

The Coast Miwok viewed the strangers' gifts with fear and refused to accept them. At the same time, they offered gifts of baskets, food, and ritual objects. The Miwok men showed awe and reverence toward the strangers, but the Native women tore at their cheeks and upper chests, cried and shrieked, and threw themselves on the rocky ground as they walked among the young Englishmen. The English left after five weeks, still baffled by the odd reception they had received.

The mystery of the Indians' peculiar behavior was solved when the Coast Miwok revealed their beliefs. The group believed that the land of the dead lay to the west, directly beyond the area Drake had come from. The Miwok thought that Drake and his men were dead ancestors. The Miwok refused their gifts because they were strictly forbidden to take anything from the land of the dead. The women were simply exhibiting mourning behavior.

Like the Coast Miwok, the English interpreted this meeting with their own misconceptions. The records referred to the headman of the local Indians as a "king," when no such role existed. The English claimed that this "king" gladly surrendered all of "his" territory and authority to the English king, halfway around the world. Finally, the English concluded that the Miwok regarded them as "gods."

1582–98 ◆ Spanish began settlement of New Mexico

Spanish expeditions began to enter what is now eastern New Mexico. Although they were at first driven back by Pueblo and Apache Indians, by 1598 a Spanish colony was established at San Juan Pueblo, in northern New Mexico.

1585-1607 ◆ Roanoke

In 1585 Sir Walter Raleigh founded an English colony on Roanoke Island, in present-day North Carolina, but the settlement did not survive. What happened to the English settlers at the Roanoke colony remains a mystery.

1588 ◆ Fur monopoly granted

King Henry III of France granted a fur trade monopoly to nephews of Jacques Cartier. Indians found that Europeans were interested in *castor gras* (greasy beaver), beaver skins that have lost their hair after having been used as clothing for a year or two. Europeans sought castor gras to make felt.

1603-07 ◆ Champlain established trading post

By the time French trader Samuel de Champlain arrived in what is now eastern Canada, the villages of Stadacona (near present-day Quebec) and Hochelaga (near present-day Montreal), discovered by Jacques Cartier, had disappeared. *(Also see entry dated 1535-36: Cartier searched for Saguenay.)* Champlain established Port Royal, a year-round trading base on the Bay of Fundy, a large bay separating the modern-day Canadian provinces of Nova Scotia and New Brunswick. There he traded with the Huron and the Algonkian-speaking peoples of Canada.

The Algonkian peoples included the Cree, Innu, Maliseet, Micmac, and Ojibway. These peoples shared many ways of life. They usually lived in small bands and moved about often. Most societies were egalitarian, meaning power was shared equally among the members and no one person was extremely powerful.

Because the Algonkian people moved about often, their housing was simple and portable. The structures in which they lived came to be known by the

A painting of a Micmac encampment. The Micmac were among the earliest Indian groups to meet the European traders.

Algonkian word *wigwam*. Birchbark provided the ideal cover for wigwams, although moose or caribou hide was often used. The covers could be rolled up and carried between camps, then quickly stretched over a dome-shaped framework of poles. Birchbark also provided lightweight cover for the canoes that were used for travel in the summer. For winter travel, snowshoes were used.

The Algonkian peoples believed they should show respect for the animals they hunted. In their view, the hunter's skill was not enough—the animal had to offer itself to the hunter to be killed. Only if they performed ceremonies properly would nature cooperate and give them what they needed to survive. After large game was killed, feasts were held to celebrate and honor the animal. Care was taken with the bones so the animal spirits would not be offended and thus avoid the hunters in the future. Animal skulls were hung from trees, and special platforms were built to keep them out of the reach of dogs. Rituals were performed to discover where game was located, or to learn whether anything would be caught during the hunt.

All Algonkian groups had shamans. Shamans were spiritual leaders who could cure diseases or foretell the future. A common ritual was the "shaking tent." Here the violent movements of a small shelter announced the arrival of spirits to assist the shaman in his work. *(Also see entries dated 1608: Champlain founded New France; and 1609: Fur trade began.)*

1607 ✦ English settlement in Virginia

The British Virginia Company, an English trading company, established a settlement at Jamestown in present-day Virginia. The colony was formed on the land of the Pamunkey Indians, a part of the Powhatan Confederacy. The Powhatan confederacy was a group of 27 tribes with a total population of more than 10,000.

The English, like other Europeans, traveled to America to use its resources and gain wealth. The Jamestown colonists gathered rocks they believed contained gold. The gold turned out to be pyrite or "fools gold," and the English tried to find other ways to become rich.

Wahunsonacock, the leader of the Powhatan Confederacy—referred to simply as Powhatan ("Falls of the River") by the English—was friendly to the colonizers. The Indians saved the Englishmen from starvation during the colony's first winter by giving them bread, corn, fish, and other food.

The English repaid this kindness by demanding that the Indians become English subjects and pay them an annual tribute of corn. John Smith was the leader of the colonists. His unfriendly policies caused conflict with many Native American peoples. Powhatan helped the colonists at first, but after a few years he became angry with them. He asked, "Why will you destroy us who supply you with food? What can you get by war?" Powhatan did not understand how important becoming rich was to the English. *(Also see entries dated 1609: Fur trade began; and 1613-14: Marriage of Pocahontas and John Rolfe.)*

1609 ✦ Fur trade began

Henry Hudson, sailing for the Netherlands, opened the fur trade in New Netherlands (present-day New York) with the Hackensack, Lenape, Manhattan, Mohican, Munsee, and Wappinger tribes. In the fur trade Indians sold beaver, deer, and other skins to the Europeans in exchange for manufactured goods, especially guns, hoes, and hatchets. The Europeans wanted furs to sell in Europe for coats, hats, and leather. After a few years of trading with the Europeans, many Indian

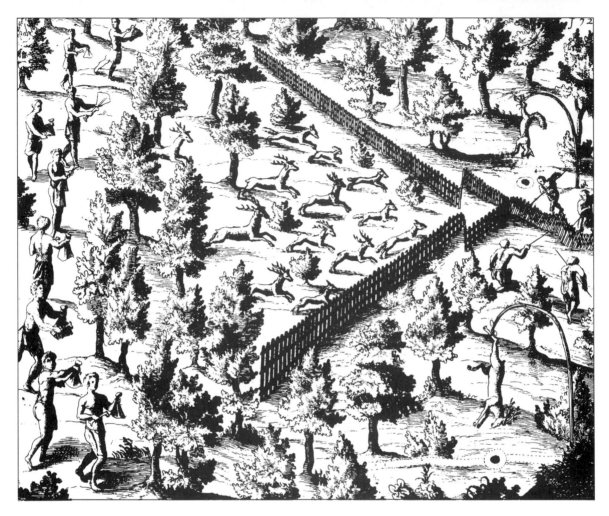

Indian method of hunting deer, from *Les Voyages du Sr. de Champlain,* c. 1615-1618.

tribes quit producing their own goods. Some groups came to depend on the fur trade to supply even their most basic needs, such as food.

1609 ◆ Huron signed trade agreement

A group of Huron Indians, an Iroquoian-speaking people, and the Algonkian traveled to Quebec and signed a trade agreement with Champlain and the French.

The Huron were one tribe of the Ontario Iroquoian, along with the Petun and Neutral, of Canada. All three groups were confederacies (or groups) of separate tribes linked by a common council. Villages were run by local councils. One council was in charge of feasts, ceremonies, and other peaceful activities, while the other was dedicated to matters of war. Councils allowed everyone present to give his or her opinion. An effort was always made to reach agreement among the members before a decision was formed.

The Huron lived in longhouses in several palisaded (well-defended) villages in the region between Lake Simcoe and Lake Huron. The villagers grew beans, corn, squash, and some sunflowers and tobacco in neighboring fields. The Huron engaged in trade, exchanging their agricultural products for dried fish and meat produced by hunter-gatherers in the north. The Huron language was the main language of trade.

The groups within the confederacies celebrated feasts, dances, and games together. Lacrosse was often played by teams from different villages. Lacrosse is played on a field by two teams of ten players each, who use a long-handled stick with a webbed pouch to maneuver a ball into the opposing team's goal. It was a popular sport, although it was played so roughly that it could result in injuries.

The most important ceremony was the Feast of the Dead, held every ten years or so. At this time the remains of all who had died since the last Feast of the Dead were removed from their temporary graves. They were reburied in a common pit, with feasting and rituals to honor them.

Warfare shaped much of the lives of the Huron. Before contact with Europeans, wars were fought for revenge and for gaining personal status. Later they were fought over access to fur-bearing animals and trade routes. Trophies of enemies who were killed were taken back to the villages. Captured enemies were also taken back, and some became part of the society. This was an important method of replacing individuals lost in battle. Other captives were tortured to death in public spectacles. *(Also see entries dated 1603-07: Champlain established trading post; and 1615: Native migration.)*

1609 ♦ John Smith captured

John Smith, leader of Jamestown colony, was captured by members of the Powhatan Confederacy because it was believed that Smith had participated in a raid on an Indian village. Legend has it that Pocahontas, Powhatan's young daughter, talked to her father and prevented Smith's execution. Captain Smith was released and allowed to return to Jamestown. *(Also see entries dated 1607: English settlement in Virginia; and 1613-14: Marriage of Pocahontas and John Rolfe.)*

1610-1710 ♦ Slave trade

Trade between southeast Indians and the English began to involve the capture and sale of Indian slaves. The English, who wanted slaves for their plantations, gave guns and other goods to Indians who would go with them on slave raids to the interior Indian nations (those living farther inland).

French artist's view of American Indians in an illustration to *Les Voyages du Sr. de Champlain,* c. 1615-1618.

However, Indians did not make particularly good slaves. Knowing the land better than the English, they escaped easily. After 1700 the English began to take Indian slaves to the Caribbean islands where it was harder for them to escape. Then the English began to import slaves from Africa to work on the plantations.

1613-14 ♦ Marriage of Pocahontas and John Rolfe

Pocahontas was captured by English settlers and held hostage. During this time she learned English and became a Christian, changing her name to Rebecca. In 1614 she married John Rolfe, an Englishman who began the European tobacco industry in North America. In 1616 Pocahontas and her husband made a widely publicized trip to England. Pocahontas provided good publicity for the English

Ætatis suæ 21. Aº. 1616.

A portrait of Pocahontas made in London in 1616, one year before her sudden death.

colonists. She was offered as proof that the struggling colony could survive and that it maintained good Indian relations. For Pocahontas, however, the trip proved deadly—she died a year later of a European disease. *(Also see entry dated 1609: John Smith captured.)*

1613-14 ◆ Tobacco growing

Conflicts between the Powhatan and the English increased as the colonists began to grow tobacco. Tobacco growing required new land every five to seven years because the plant used up the soil's nutrients. Because of this the colonists sought more land in inland Indian hunting areas or lands that Indians had already cleared and used for farming.

1615 ✦ Huron formed trade network

The Huron formed a trade network by serving as the middlemen for trade between the French in the east and western Native American groups. The Huron would receive furs from Native Americans and trade them to the French for European goods. This trade made the Hurons very wealthy.

To maintain their control of the fur trade, the Huron were forced to engage in warfare with other tribes. Their main rival was the Five Nations of the Iroquois. Champlain supported the Huron in early battles against the Iroquois, turning the mighty Five Nations Confederacy against the French.

1615 ✦ Native migration

The confederacy of Algonkian-speaking nations, forced off their land by colonial settlers and in search of good fur hunting areas, continued to move from the Atlantic Coast to the Lake Michigan and Lake Superior area. *(Also see entry dated 1609: Huron signed trade agreement.)*

1618-31 ✦ First Virginia War

Powhatan died in 1618. His brother, Opechancanough, became the new leader of the Powhatan Confederacy. In 1622 Opechancanough attacked the English, almost driving them from Virginia. The English Crown took over the Jamestown colony and Virginia, providing aid and protection to the settlers.

The first Virginia War lasted ten years with many deaths among Natives and colonists. The territory of the Chickahominy nation, an ally nation within the Powhatan Confederacy, was devastated by colonial attacks throughout the 1620s. The Native population in Virginia began to decline significantly, mostly because of disease, warfare, and westward movement. *(Also see entry dated 1644-46: Second Virginia War.)*

1620 ✦ Arrival of the Pilgrims

The Pilgrims arrived aboard the *Mayflower* at Plymouth, Massachusetts. Before landing, they signed an agreement, the Mayflower Compact, that called for self-rule. The Pilgrims barely survived their first winter in Massachusetts, but were helped by friendly Indians.

Massasoit, a principal leader of the Wampanoag people, encouraged friendship with English settlers. As leader of the Wampanoag, Massasoit controlled a number of Indian groups that occupied lands in present-day Massachusetts. He negotiated friendly relations with the recently arrived Pilgrims and later with the

Puritans. As early as 1621, with the aid of Squanto, a Wampanoag who spoke English, Massasoit carried on communications with the Pilgrims at their Plymouth settlement. Massasoit helped the settlers in a number of ways, including giving them land and advice on farming and hunting. Massasoit eventually came to oppose the English settlers and his son, Philip, turned to war in 1675–76. Massasoit died in 1661.

1621 ◆ Tisquantum (Squanto) and Thanksgiving

One of the Native Americans who helped the Pilgrims was Tisquantum, more commonly known as Squanto. He was captured by the English sometime between 1605 and 1614 and sold as a slave in Spain. He escaped and returned home, where he discovered that his village had been destroyed by disease. Tisquantum lived with the Wampanoag and their chief, Massasoit, who extended his people's authority over much of present-day Massachusetts and Rhode Island. Tisquantum had learned English during his travels.

Like many other Native Americans, Tisquantum aided the colonists, showing them where to hunt and fish, and how to grow and prepare native crops such as beans, corn, and squash. After their disastrous first winter, the Pilgrims learned quickly from the Indians' lessons. In the fall of 1621 the Pilgrims invited Massasoit to a feast to give thanks. He attended with 90 people. When the Pilgrims did not have enough food, Massasoit asked his people to provide food as well. This was the first Thanksgiving. *(Also see entry dated 1620: Arrival of the Pilgrims.)*

1626 ◆ Manhattan Island sold

Peter Minuit, governor of the Dutch colony New Netherland (later renamed New York when the British took it from the Dutch), traded 60 guilders of goods—legend says worth 24 dollars—for Manhattan Island, part of present-day New York City.

1627 ◆ New France Company chartered

The Company of New France was chartered by the French government to colonize New France (areas in Canada settled by the French) and further develop the fur trade with Indians. The fur trade was the major factor in French relations with Canadian Native groups in the 1600s and 1700s. The French interest was primarily economic—they profited a great deal from the furs the Indians could deliver. The French, who did not acknowledge Indian rights to hold land, had never negotiated treaties with Canadian Indians. Relations between the French and aboriginal (Native) people of Canada varied from open hostility to shared purpose and friendliness, but throughout their history, the French and the aboriginal Canadians treated each other as separate, sovereign nations. The French never took title to aboriginal lands in Canada.

The Franciscan method of teaching the Indians by pictures. From an engraving based on Fray Diego Valdés, o.F.M., in his *Rhetorica Christiana,* Rome, 1579.

1628-29 ♦ Spanish colonies in the Southwest

When the Spanish began to colonize the American Southwest, they forcefully controlled the village peoples, forbidding them to practice their ceremonies and rituals. Many Pueblos were forced to work on the ranches and farms of the Spanish officers and upper class.

Spanish missionaries demanded that Native Americans convert, or change their beliefs, to Christianity and abandon their traditional religions. Young Pueblos were forced into the Spanish army, whose main function was to make slave raids into nearby areas.

In 1629 Spanish missionaries began to try to convert the Zuni and Hopi tribes to Christianity. The Spanish were opposed by Native religious leaders and driven away.

1630 ✦ Puritans arrived

The Puritans (a Protestant religious group) arrived in Massachusetts. The Puritans believed that they were on a mission from God to establish a perfect Christian society. Puritan minister Cotton Mather called the Indians the "accursed seed of Canaan" and preached that they should be made subject to Christian rule. Some Puritans believed that God had sent the diseases that wiped out the majority of the Native American population in the Northeast in order to clear the lands so that the Puritans could settle them.

1631-42 ✦ Roger Williams and Indian rights

Roger Williams of the Massachusetts colony argued that the royal charter for the colony illegally took Indian lands. Williams urged a humane policy toward Indians. In 1636 he founded Rhode Island and insisted that settlers there buy land from Indians. In 1642 Williams's Indian-English dictionary was published in London. *(Also see entry dated 1630: Puritans arrived.)*

1632 ✦ Jesuits began missionary efforts

The Jesuits, members of a Roman Catholic religious order, began to conduct missionary efforts among the Huron and Algonkian in Canada. The Jesuits later set up agricultural settlements and schools for Native Americans. *(Also see entry dated 1568: Jesuit Indian school organized.)*

1634 ✦ Nicolet explored the Northeast

A Frenchman, Jean Nicolet, traveled up the Ottawa River to Georgian Bay and then to Sault Sainte Marie and Wisconsin. Meeting different Algonkian-speaking peoples, he learned of many powerful societies. The Winnebago, for example, had over 3,000 warriors and already traded European goods with the Huron, Ottawa, and Nipissing.

1634-37 ✦ Pequot War

The Pequot, a tribe known for its warlike ways and disliked by many Indian tribes, lived in what is now Connecticut. In 1634 Indians (probably the neighboring Narragansett) killed some Puritans who were hunting for Indian slaves. In retaliation Puritans claimed absolute rule over the Pequot and demanded

Pequot land and the surrender of the killers. The Pequot agreed to these terms. Two years later another Puritan was killed by Indians and the English again demanded the surrender of the killer. This time the Pequot refused and war erupted. The settlers raised an army consisting of Puritans, Pilgrims, Mohican, and Narragansetts. This army attacked and set fire to the Pequot fort, killing as many as 700 Pequot men, women, and children.

1635 ✦ First Indian school established in New France

The Jesuits, a Catholic religious order, established the first school for Indians in New France. Instruction was in French, Latin, Huron, and Montagnais. *(Also see entries dated 1568: Jesuit Indian school organized; and 1632: Jesuits begin missionary efforts.)*

1639–62 ✦ Taos Indians abandoned New Mexico pueblo

The Taos Indians abandoned their pueblo in present-day New Mexico and fled to live with the Apaches in what is now western Kansas, where they built a new pueblo. Some were taken back by the Spaniards before 1642, but others stayed until 1662. The Taos introduced the use of horses, which they brought with them from the Southwest, to the central plains by 1640 at the latest.

1640 ✦ Five Nations searched for new beaver supply

The Five Nations of the Iroquois Confederacy were no longer able to supply their trade requirements by hunting and trapping on their home territory in upstate New York because they had exhausted the beaver supply in their area. The Five Nations had come to depend on trade with the Dutch to supply knives, axes, cloth, beads, and guns and powder.

The Iroquois tried to negotiate trade and diplomatic agreements with the Huron, but the French prevented the two sides from reaching an agreement because they wanted to keep control of the fur trade through their Huron allies. The competition between the Iroquois and the Huron would lead to conflict, and eventually war. The French began selling guns to Huron who had converted to Christianity. The Iroquois, angered at the French for selling arms to their enemies, began unlimited war on the French. *(Also see entries dated 1648-51: Beaver Wars; 1653: Five Nations made peace with France; and 1662-80: Five Nations of the Iroquois League under attack.)*

1642 ✦ Ville Marie founded

Ville Marie (present-day Montreal) was founded as a missionary outpost. It soon developed into a trade center.

1644-46 ✦ Second Virginia War

The Powhatan Confederacy began a second war against the Virginia colony. After the war of 1622, the Indians tried to live in peace with the settlers, but the

English expanded onto Indian lands. The Powhatan went to war to prevent the colonists from taking more Indian territory.

Opechancanough, now old and feeble, was carried to the battlefield, where he wanted to die a warrior's death rather than surrender to the English. After two years of warfare, the Indians and colonists negotiated an agreement. The Treaty of 1646 prohibited English land expansion, but the Indians were left with only a portion of their former area. Indians were also required to provide an annual supply of beaver pelts to the colonial government. By 1649 the English colonists were already disregarding the treaty and moving farther into Indian territory. *(Also see entry dated 1618-31: First Virginia War.)*

1648-51 ◆ Beaver Wars
The Five Nations (Iroquois), with Dutch support and guns, attacked the Huron and their trading allies in order to gain a reliable supply of beaver pelts. By 1650 the Huron trade empire was destroyed by the Five Nations and the entire Huron population was scattered. Some survivors became

Indians Trading Furs, by C. W. Jefferys.

members of neighboring groups, including the tribes of the Iroquois Confederacy; others moved throughout the Great Lakes area, where they became known as Wyandot (also known as Wyandotte or Wendat, derived from Ouendat, their own name for themselves).

The Five Nations then attacked the Indian groups of the interior, pushing them farther into the Great Lakes regions of present-day Michigan and Wisconsin. The Ottawa now replaced the Huron as the middlemen between Indian nations of the Great Lakes and the French. The French also began to trade directly with many Indian groups. *(Also see entries dated 1640: Five Nations searched for new beaver supply; 1653: Five Nations made peace with France; and 1662-80: Five Nations of the Iroquois under attack.)*

1650 ◆ Cheyenne migration began
The Cheyenne, probably living in present-day southern Ontario or Quebec, were forced to migrate westward because of the expanding Iroquois trade empire.

1653 ◆ Five Nations made peace with France
The Iroquois, having established themselves as the dominant power in the St. Lawrence and eastern Great Lakes regions, no longer had reason to fight the

French. In the fall a partial peace was agreed to, but many Iroquois were still concerned about French alliances with their enemies.

1660 ✦ Chippewa–Sioux Wars

The Chippewa (Ojibway) who lived in the upper Great Lakes region started to move west, armed with guns and trade goods. Pushed by colonial and Iroquois expansion, the Chippewa invaded Sioux territory in present-day Minnesota. After much fighting with the Chippewa, many Sioux moved onto the plains in the 1700s, where they adopted the buffalo-hunting horse culture for which they are well known in U.S. history. Before this time, the Sioux were a settled agricultural (farming) people living in the woodlands east of the Great Plains area. *(Also see entry dated Late 1700s: Sioux moved to the Plains.)*

1662–80 ✦ Five Nations of the Iroquois League under attack

During this time the Confederacy of Five Nations of the Iroquois was engaged in almost constant warfare with the Erie, Ottawa, Wyandot, and Algonkian tribes. At first the Iroquois were successful, almost driving the French from what is now Canada. Eventually, though, the Iroquois's opponents, supported by the French, began to weaken the Iroquois empire. By 1680 the Iroquois were pushed out of the Great Lakes area. *(Also see entries dated 1640: Five Nations searched for new beaver supply; and 1648-51: Beaver Wars.)*

With the colonists of New France threatened by continual Iroquois attacks, French troops attacked Iroquois villages in 1666. The attack killed few Indians but destroyed Iroquois villages and crops. The two sides then negotiated a truce that lasted ten years.

1670 ✦ Hudson's Bay Company chartered

The Hudson's Bay Company was chartered by the English. This company would control trade with Native Americans for the English and set up many trading bases in various areas of Canada.

1671 ✦ Puritans established reservations

The Puritans established 14 reservations in New England for Native Americans that restricted Indian rights and forced them off their lands. Native Americans who lived on the reservations were ruled by English law, were forced to accept Christianity, and could not buy guns or whiskey. *(Also see entry dated 1630: Puritans arrived.)*

1671-73 ✦ French forts established

The French established forts on the Great Lakes for the purposes of defense, trade, missions, and diplomacy. Competing for furs with the English Hudson's Bay Company, the French increased their sale of firearms to their Indian allies.

1671-80 ◆ Apaches migrated to the Southwest

Apaches began migrating to the Southwest from the southern Plains after disease killed many of their horses. They, along with the Navajo, raided Spanish settlements and Indian pueblos and stole sheep, horses, and trade goods. The Apache were well equipped with guns and horses and were able to challenge Spanish armed forces. The Apache also depended on hunting and fishing for their survival.

1675-76 ◆ King Philip's War

Wampanoag leader Metacom, known to the English as King Philip, tried to put a stop to the abuses of the Puritans by gathering an army from many area tribes. King Philip's army attacked more than half the English settlements in New England. Weakened by major epidemics, even the allied Indian forces were not strong enough to win the war, although they held their own against Puritan forces for a time. The Puritan government executed Metacom. His wife, son, and hundreds of his followers were sold into slavery. Many of Metacom's allies fled. By the end of King Philip's War, the few remaining Indians in the New England colonies were living in small towns and had adopted Christianity. The colonists called these groups "Praying Indians," and their towns were often called "Praying Towns."

1675-77 ◆ Bacon's Rebellion

A third major war erupted between Indians and settlers in Virginia. The colonists, led by Nathaniel Bacon in a rebellion to free Virginia colony from English rule, also made war on the Susquehannock, the Rappahanock, and other southeast tribes. The English defeated the rebellion, but not before Bacon's army killed and enslaved many Native Americans. The Indians lost heavily in the war. The peace treaty signed in 1677 forced the Indians to accept English law and opened more of their land to colonial settlement. *(Also see entries dated 1618-31: First Virginia War; and 1644-46: Second Virginia War.)*

1677–1731 ◆ Shawnee migrations and regroupings

The Shawnee probably lived in what is now northern Kentucky and southern Ohio before European contact. During the late 1600s Chickasaw and Cherokee slave raiding and fur trading expeditions forced the Shawnee to retreat from their homeland. Some Shawnee migrated south to Georgia to live on the Savannah River, which is named after them, while others moved to western Virginia and Pennsylvania. Others joined the Creek nation in Alabama, where they established a permanent village.

Late 1600s ◆ Europeans contacted Cherokee

Europeans first visited the Cherokee in the southern Appalachian Mountains. Cherokee villages were located in mountain river valleys where there was space for houses, council houses, and farm fields.

An engraving of William Penn, founder of Pennsylvania, concluding a treaty with the Delaware Indians.

The Cherokee were a matrilineal society. Their fields were controlled by the Cherokee women. Women who had great influence or power became known as Beloved Women. Beloved Women often worked behind the scenes to help shape major decisions. A woman could take her husband's place in war, in which case she was given the title War Woman.

1680-96 ◆ Pueblo revolt
Pueblo spiritual leader Pope led his people in a rebellion that forced the Spanish and their Indian allies to move to present-day El Paso, Texas. Pope claimed that the spirits told him to drive away the Spanish and help the Pueblo return to their traditional life. But Spanish military forces regained control, and by 1696 many Pueblos had left their villages to join the Navajo bands to the north. The Pueblo who remained under Spanish rule were forced to convert to Catholicism (accept it as their religion). They were also forced to work on the ranches of Spanish officers and other wealthy people.

1682 ◆ Pennsylvania Colony and Delaware Treaty
English Quaker leader William Penn purchased the site of present-day Philadelphia, Pennsylvania. The treaty was negotiated with a leading Delaware chief, sometimes called Tammany. A long period of peaceful relations began between Quakers and the Indians.

1683 ◆ Lacrosse described
French missionaries describe an Ojibway (Chippewa) sport called *baggataway*

(lacrosse). Lacrosse is played on a field by two teams of ten players each, in which players use a long-handled stick with a webbed pouch to maneuver a ball into the opposing team's goal.

Ojibway shelter frame.

1684-88 ♦ Five Nations neutrality policy

The Five Nations of the Iroquois Confederacy, defeated in its attempts to control the fur trade, decided to change its policy concerning the English and the French. In the past the Iroquois had supported the English, but now they would not take sides with either of the two European powers. This policy, however, would not bring peace to the Five Nations. They would be involved in warfare for the next 100 years.

1685 ♦ The Chippewa, or Ojibway

At this time the Ottawa controlled two-thirds of the fur trade with the French. The Ottawa were one tribe of the Ojibway, or Chippewa as they were known in the United States. The Ojibway were an Algonkian-speaking group who lived in many regions around the Great Lakes. The groups were comprised of small, independent bands, including the Saulteaux, Ottawa, Nipissing, and Mississauga. They did not consider themselves part of one large group. However, their Algonkian-based lan-

EUROPEAN WARS IN AMERICA

King William's War, which started in 1689, began a series of colonial wars that lasted until the end of the War of 1812. During this period of more than 125 years, Indian nations attempted to maintain trade relations with one or more of the European combatants—the English, French, and Spanish—or the newly formed United States. Indian nations hoped these alliances would help them maintain their political independence and keep their territory. The European nations welcomed Native American support because it was cheaper to use Indian warriors than to bring in soldiers from their home countries. These alliances turned out to be disastrous for Native American peoples, because even when they were on the winning side they were still forced to give up their land.

War	Year(s)
King William's War	1689-97
Queen Ann's War	1702-13
King George's War	1744-48
French and Indian War	1754-63
American Revolutionary War	1775-83
War of 1812	1812-13

guages were similar enough that they understood each other, and they held common traditions.

The Ojibway groups lived by hunting, fishing, and gathering plants. Larger groups met seasonally at good fishing locations, such as the rapids at Sault Sainte Marie on Lake Superior. The shallow lakes of the area provided wild rice, an important part of the Ojibway diet. Maple sugar was used as a seasoning for a wide range of foods. Some of the southern groups farmed or traded fish and furs for farm produce.

1690-1700 ◆ Settlers took Indian lands

In Virginia, settlers sought ways to acquire still more Indian lands. The Virginia government continuously broke existing treaties with Indian nations. Although the British Crown often upheld Indian rights, colonists and Virginia officials kept taking over Indian lands.

1690-1701 ◆ Métis in Canada

The Métis of Canada were a group of people who descended from the intermarriages between the French and the Chippewa (Ojibway) Indians. The French word *métis* referred to mixed-blood people, especially those of mixed European and American Indian ancestry.

Aside from gaining the usual advantages of marriage, the traders benefitted from these marriages in their work. Trade was made easier by having relationships with the Native people. Native women often acted as interpreters. They also performed skilled tasks such as making snowshoes, drying meat, and dressing furs. Male children of these marriages often became traders, and a distinct group of people with mixed heritage began to emerge. *(Also see entry dated Mid-1700s: Métis migrated to Plains.)*

1700 ◆ Spanish missions

Native Americans influenced the Spanish in many ways, particularly with their foods, natural resources, and architecture. In return, Indians acquired horses, cattle, sheep, mules, and other livestock. In California and Texas, Indians became skilled cowboys and cowgirls. They also learned to grow wheat, commonly used to make bread. Some Indians learned the new Christian religion, which spread rapidly among tribes. Spanish priests established missions from the Atlantic to the Pacific. Indians supplied the labor to build the beautiful structures so admired today.

Life on missions was hard. Indians often died from inadequate diet, disease, unsanitary conditions, and overwork. Sometimes they received no treatment for injuries or disease. When Indians refused to work, priests or Christian Indians whipped the people, including women and children. When families fled the missions, soldiers hunted them down and forced them to return. *(Also see entry dated 1769: First mission established in California.)*

1710 ✦ Four kings visited London

Hailed and celebrated as Indian kings, four Mohawk diplomats visited London. There they received royal treatment, gaining a celebrity status unknown among previous Indian visitors to Europe and even meeting with Queen Anne before their return to North America.

INDIAN WARS

Not only did Native Americans fight against and with Europeans, they also fought among themselves in the 1700s. There were many causes for these wars. Native American tribes fought each other over land, trade, and other long-time arguments. They also fought each other in European conflicts. The Iroquois Confederacy, one of the strongest Native American nations, which controlled much of the fur trade, was constantly at war between 1636 and the end of the American Revolution in 1783. These wars among themselves often weakened the military powers of Native American groups, making it easier for European and American armies to defeat them. The result of these conflicts between tribes was usually the migration, or movement to a new homeland, of the losing Indian tribe.

1713 ✦ Micmac resisted the English

The Micmac and Maliseet tribes of what is now eastern Canada refused to recognize the terms of the Treaty of Utrecht (April 4, 1713), by which the French gave Micmac and Maliseet homeland to the English. The English refused to give annual gifts to the tribes as the French had done, so the Micmac decided to resist their takeover of this area. *(Also see entries dated November 22, 1752: Halifax Treaty; and January 26, 1841: Micmac appealed to Queen Victoria.)*

July 1717 ✦ Chipewyan became trade middlemen

The establishment of a Hudson's Bay Company post at the mouth of the Churchill River enabled the Chipewyan to establish themselves as middlemen to other Athapaskan, or Dene, groups that lived in the Western Subarctic area.

Athapaskan tribes spoke 20 closely related languages. The three major Athapaskan tribes were the Beaver, Chipewyan, and Tahltan. Forests covered the western subarctic area, which was crossed by numerous rivers and dotted with lakes. Caribou and moose were among the most important game animals for the Athapaskans. Bison were also hunted in the southern areas, and mountain goats and sheep were hunted in the Cordillera Mountains. Smaller animals, such as the snowshoe hare, were also important food sources. At certain times of the

Detail from Indian encampment on Lake Huron. Art Gallery of Ontario.

year, great numbers of waterfowl could be caught. The lakes and rivers provided whitefish, lake trout, grayling, and other fish. Groups in the western areas, where rivers flowed to the Pacific, had access to bountiful runs of salmon.

Athapaskan societies were generally small. They moved frequently, following game across a large area. In general, population density was low. Groups did not usually have formal chiefs, although certain people often took leadership roles for specific tasks, such as hunting, trade, or war. Social relations were flexible, and personal freedom was highly valued.

Snowshoes, sleds, and toboggans were essential to winter travel. In summer, people traveled along the lakes and rivers in bark-covered canoes. Housing differed among Athapaskan groups, but most used simple hide-covered structures shaped like cones or domes. More substantial winter houses were used in a few areas. *(Also see entry dated 1730: Cree became trade middlemen.)*

1720 ◆ First Indian school created
The first permanent Indian school was created in Williamsburg, Virginia.

1722 ◆ Six Nations Confederacy formed
The Tuscarora concluded an agreement with the Iroquois Five Nations to form the Six Nations Confederacy. The Tuscarora moved to the region from North Carolina in 1714 after being displaced by war, conflict over trade debts, and European agricultural (farming) expansion. Although they came from a differ-

Miniature model showing Natchez life, with a house for corn storage on the left and a temple mound in the back.

ent part of the continent, the Tuscarora found that their language was closely related to some of the Iroquois languages.

1729 ◆ Destruction of the Natchez nation

The Natchez, a Mississippian culture governed by a sacred chieftain, the Great Sun, rebelled against the French. The Natchez wiped out the French at Natchez Plantation in Louisiana, but the French and their Indian allies destroyed Natchez villages and captured the Great Sun. The chief and many of his supporters were sold into slavery in the Caribbean.

1730 ◆ Cree became trade middlemen

The Cree took over as trade middlemen between the Athapaskan people and the Hudson's Bay Company. The Cree were well supplied with guns and other European-made goods by the English. This Cree advantage in warfare caused heavy losses of life among the Chipewyan, who fought the Cree to maintain their trading role. Soon the Chipewyan decided to abandon the fur trade and returned to their previous way of life. *(Also see entry dated July 1717: Chipewyan became trade middlemen.)*

1740-1805 ◆ Russians explored the Northwest Coast

The first Russian explorers, led by Vitus Bering, sailed to Alaska and explored the entire coastline. The Russians met and traded with the Aleut of the Aleutian Islands for sea otter pelts and sealskins. The Russians established colonies and traded guns, powder, lead, pots and pans, knives, fishhooks, beads, and cloth for fur.

The Aleut depended on the sea for their survival. The abundant sea life included sea urchins, clams, octopus, fish, sea otters, seals, and whales. These were used for food, clothing, and homes. Birds and their eggs, berries, wild rice, celery, and other plants were also part of the Aleutian diet. The men were skilled hunters on the open sea and used two-person skin boats (baidarka) for hunting seals and whales.

Aleutian villages were situated along the coast, allowing easy access to the sea. They were small, usually with only 100 to 200 inhabitants. Two to five families lived in houses called *barbaras,* which were built partly underground.

The family was the primary grouping in Aleut society, serving as the basis for social relations, economics (the way people supported themselves and accumulated wealth), warfare, and political relations. Aleuts were a matrilineal society, with inheritance following the mother's line of relatives. Children were trained and disciplined by the mother's family. Men were responsible for hunting and the care of tools and boats. Women cared for the home and gathered food along the beaches and shallow waters.

Traditional society was loosely divided into groups of nobles, commoners, and slaves captured in wars with other villages. The most respected hunters, those with years of experience and great skill, became Aleut chiefs. However, chiefs had little real power and decisions required the agreement of everyone. Warfare was not uncommon among Aleut groups. Wars were fought for a variety of reasons—revenge, the capture of slaves, or trade conflicts.

In 1766 the Russians declared control over the Aleutian Islands, but in fact Russian traders and hunters generally acted on their own, with few restrictions from their government. The Russians brought epidemic diseases to the Native people and murdered many. It is estimated that 90 percent of the Native population was lost to disease or murder. Those Indians who survived were often forced into slave labor. The Russians used the men as hunters on the open sea or as warriors.

Mid-1700s ✦ Comanche moved to southern Plains

During the early 1700s, the Comanche moved to New Mexico from present-day Wyoming. By the mid-1700s, the Comanche had gained control of the horse and gun trade on the southern Plains. They had become the most powerful bison-hunting tribe in the area.

Mid-1700s ✦ Métis migrated to Canadian Plains

A large "mixed blood," or Métis, population in Canada had settled around the Great Lakes by this time. As fur-bearing animals became scarce and settlers moved in from the east, many of the Métis moved westward to the Plains.

The center of Métis culture formed at the point where the Red and Assiniboine rivers joined (near present-day Winnipeg, Manitoba, Canada). The Métis conducted communal bison hunts. Once the hunters located herds, they killed

the bison from horseback. The meat was cut into strips, dried, pounded into coarse powder, mixed with melted fat, and sewn into hide bags. This was called pemmican, an important part of the fur trade economy and a necessary winter food for many of the trading posts of the distant Northwest. *(Also see entry dated 1690-1701: Settlers took Indian lands.)*

Hunters in the western regions of the Plains using horses to drive large herds of buffalo over "buffalo jumps."

November 22, 1752 ◆ Halifax Treaty
The Micmac and the British signed a peace treaty that brought Micmac resistance temporarily to an end. The British agreed to give annual gifts to the Micmac and to recognize Micmac hunting and fishing rights. *(Also see entries dated 1713: Micmac resisted the English; and January 26, 1841: Micmac appealed to Queen Victoria.)*

1754 ◆ Albany Plan
Benjamin Franklin, a prominent citizen and statesman from Pennsylvania, proposed a plan of union for the British colonies. Franklin had visited the Iroquois Confederacy several times and suggested using their model to unify the colonies. The plan failed in 1754, but later formed the basis for the Articles of Confederation, the first laws of U.S. government, and the U.S. Constitution.

1754-63 ◆ French and Indian War
The French and Indian War began in 1754 when the European colonies went to war over lands along the Ohio River. Different Native American groups sided with both the English and the French colonial powers. At first the war went well for the French and their Spanish and Indian allies, but eventually the French lost all of their lands in North America, including Canada and the Illinois-Mississippi River valleys. Indians who fought with the French then found themselves with-

out a European ally and without a supplier of arms and trade goods. The British now controlled all trade with the Indians and tried to regulate the supply of goods, including weapons and ammunition. The British also occupied the former French forts of Detroit and Chicago on lands the Indians claimed to be theirs.

1760-63 ◆ Delaware Prophet

Several prophets emerged among the Delaware people. The most important of these was known as the "militant" prophet. The militant prophet told the Delaware that the Europeans would have to be driven from North America and that the Indians must return to the customs of their ancestors if they wanted to be returned to their previous happy life. This message influenced the Ottawa leader Pontiac, who would use it to unite Indian tribes to attack the British in 1763. *(Also see entry dated 1763: Pontiac's War.)*

1763 ◆ Pontiac's War

Pontiac, a chief of the Ottawa tribe, formed an Indian confederacy, hoping to prevent the British from taking over former French lands surrounding the Great Lakes after the French and Indian War. Indian forces captured all British forts west of Niagara Falls except Fort Detroit and Fort Pitt (Pittsburgh). Pontiac was guided by the teachings of the militant prophet from the Delaware tribe who taught that the English should be driven from the American continent and that Native Americans should return to the customs of their ancestors. Pontiac ultimately failed to prevent the British from taking over the forts. *(Also see entry dated 1760-63: Delaware Prophet.)*

1763 ◆ Proclamation of 1763

King George III of England issued the Proclamation of 1763, which assigned all lands west of the Appalachian Mountains to Native Americans, while colonists were allowed to settle all land to the east. This document also restated that Native Americans had aboriginal title to their lands. This meant that they owned the land because they were the first, or original, inhabitants. Only the British Crown, not the colonists, could buy land from Indians. Many colonists ignored the act and moved onto Indian lands. Britain's promises to respect the land rights of Native peoples were not popular among colonists. In fact, the conflict between England and the colonies over Indian lands was one of the major causes of the American Revolution.

1768 ◆ Treaty of Fort Stanwix

In the Treaty of Fort Stanwix the British forced the Six Nations of the Iroquois to give up land in present-day Kentucky and Ohio. Most of this land belonged to the Shawnee, one of the six tribes that made up the Iroquois Confederacy. The

Shawnee did not agree to the treaty, weakening the unity of the Six Nations. Many Indian nations, led by the Delaware, Miami, and Shawnee, abandoned the Iroquois, claiming they were too controlled by the British.

1769 ◆ First mission established in California

The Spanish built their first mission in California in the Native village of Cosoy, later called San Diego by the Spanish. The object of this mission, and others built in the future, was not only to convert Indians to Christianity, but also to reduce the many free and independent Native societies into a mass of slave laborers. The Spanish would ultimately establish 23 missions in California that resembled the Caribbean plantations that had been so destructive to Native peoples.

Ottawa chief Pontiac smoking the calumet, or peace pipe, with British officer Robert Rogers, who is on his way to occupy Detroit.

A group of Plains Cree driving buffalo into an enclosure constructed of branches, where the buffalo were slaughtered.

By decree of Spanish law, Indians were baptized. After baptism they were called neophytes (or new members of the Catholic church) and removed from their villages into areas near the missions. Then they were put to work. At the missions, the Indians were closely controlled. Neophyte children were removed from their families at the age of five or six. They were locked in barracks and watched by colonists who wanted to teach the children without interference from their parents. Indian girls were locked up when they weren't working or attending church. They were freed upon marriage, but if they lost their husbands they were once again locked up in the barracks. *(Also see entries dated 1700: Spanish missions; and 1824: Native resistance to Spanish missions.)*

c. 1770 ◆ Horses led to development of High Plains Culture

Horses spread to most Plains Indians by 1750, drastically changing the way of life for these Native Americans. Horses could travel fast and far, and tribes who had them could raid other tribes for food rather than growing it themselves. Tribes were forced to acquire horses in order to defend themselves and to seek revenge.

With the arrival of horses, nations that had lived by farming soon turned to buffalo hunting and raiding. Warfare increased greatly. The Plains Culture (also called the High Plains Culture) emerged. It featured warrior societies, group tribal hunts, and the Sun Dance, a sacrificial ceremony intended to promote the well-being of the community. The Plains Culture Indian is one of the most common images of Native Americans in the popular culture of the United States. Western movies and novels have frequently depicted the fierce, horseback-riding Indian warriors of the Plains. However, as a way of life, the Plains culture was relatively short-lived, lasting only about 200 years, and it was not typical of the way Native American cultures had lived for centuries before.

Most Indian nations now regarded as Plains tribes originally lived farther east. These groups migrated, or moved, onto the plains after 1650, when European expansion and trade forced many Indians westward. The Iroquois in upstate New York pushed west to gain access to land with fur-bearing animals, which were necessary for trade with Europeans. The Iroquois expansion created a domino effect, as nations pushed each other farther west in their quest for fur.

March 5, 1770 ✦ Boston Massacre

The Boston Massacre occurred when the British fired into a crowd gathered outside the Boston Customs House in defiance of British policy. Crispus Attucks, a man of African American and Massachusetts Indian descent, was killed.

1773-74 ✦ Lord Dunmore's War

Angry that settlers from Virginia were moving onto their lands and sometimes murdering Indians, the Shawnee and their allies fought back to protect their territories in western Virginia and western Pennsylvania. Lord Dunmore, governor of Virginia, formed an army and fought a series of battles with Indian groups along the Virginia and Pennsylvania frontiers.

Late 1700s ✦ Sioux moved to Plains

The Sioux, forced out of their territory in present-day Minnesota by invading Chippewa, moved west to the plains. The Sioux became accomplished horse riders and buffalo hunters. They practiced the Sun Dance, a dance of sacrifice for the well-being of the community. The Sioux also began raiding the villages of farming peoples who lived along the Missouri River, such as the Mandan, Arikara, and Hidatsa. (*Also see entry dated 1660: Chippewa-Sioux Wars.*)

1774-75 ✦ Formation of the Indian Departments

During the First Continental Congress, a meeting held in Philadelphia in 1774 in which representatives from all the colonies addressed their grievances with Britain, the delegates, worried about Indian loyalties, appointed a Committee on Indian Affairs to negotiate with Native American groups. The colonists wanted the Indians either to support them in a war against the English or to agree to stay

---

SUN DANCE

The Sun Dance was an annual world renewal and purification ceremony performed in slightly different ways among the northern Plains Indian nations such as the Cheyenne, the Sioux, and the Crow. In many practices of the Sun Dance, wooden sticks tied to a pole on one end were placed under the skin of participating men's chests. The men looked at the sun and blew eagle bone whistles until they could tear themselves free. One striking aspect of the ceremony was the personal sacrifice that these men made. Through self-torture, they hoped either to give thanks to the spirit world for a blessing received, or to gain a vision that might provide spiritual insight and knowledge that would help the community.

---

out of any war. It was decided that Indian affairs would be handled by the Continental Congress, not the individual colonies. Benjamin Franklin and Patrick Henry were two of the first commissioners appointed, showing how important Indian affairs were to the new nation.

1775 ✦ American Revolution

Indian nations were faced with a difficult decision at the beginning of the American Revolution. Many believed that the British would win the war. Many Indians also believed that the colonists, who were interested in moving onto Indian land, were a greater threat to the Indians than the British government.

1775 ✦ Cheyenne received the Sacred Law

Before they moved onto the Plains, the Cheyenne lived in present-day southern Canada. Pushed west by the Iroquois, the Cheyenne were living in present-day Minnesota by the early 1700s. By the late 1700s, they were living in eastern North Dakota. Originally farmers and hunters, they also began using horses and hunting buffalo, while growing corn crops in their new homes.

According to Cheyenne tradition, at about this time the Cheyenne were granted their Sacred Law through the prophet Sweet Medicine. Sweet Medicine received the law directly from the Creator on a sacred mountain, present-day Bear Butte in South Dakota. He told the Cheyenne to form a council of 44 chiefs and gave them their most sacred bundle—four arrows and their version of the Sun Dance. Sweet Medicine also taught the Cheyenne the Sacred Arrow Bundle Dance, which renewed the relationship between the tribe and the Creator. In this relationship the Cheyenne people agreed to uphold the Sacred Law and ceremonies, and in return the Creator would preserve the Cheyenne Nation from physical and cultural destruction.

1775 ✦ Indian education

The Continental Congress gave $500 to Moors Charity School (which later became Dartmouth College). The school was run by Dr. Eleazer Wheelock. Dr. Wheelock's idea for the education of Indian children was to remove them from their families and tribes. The children were placed in schools and homes where they could be exposed to "civilized" life. Ideally, they would then return to their communities and continue to convert their own people to mainstream American ways and beliefs.

1776 ✦ Iroquois attended Independence debates

The founding fathers invited Iroquois chiefs to attend the debates on the Declaration of Independence in Philadelphia, Pennsylvania. Over a period of weeks, the Iroquois watched the new nation emerge. They gave the president of the group, John Hancock, an Iroquois name— "Karanduawn," which means "the Great Tree," the symbol of the birth of the Iroquois Confederacy.

1777-83 ◆ Iroquois Confederacy destroyed

The American Revolutionary War permanently destroyed the unity of the Iroquois Confederacy in the future United States. Some members of the Confederacy supported the British and others the Americans, while some decided not to take sides. The split lasted after the war. Between 1777 and 1800 the newly formed American government allowed various land companies to buy virtually all Iroquois lands. By 1880 the Iroquois either had left their lands to live in Canada or were relocated to small reservations in upstate New York.

1777-87 ◆ Articles of Confederation

Under the Articles of Confederation—the first U.S. laws of national government—Native American groups were treated as sovereign (independent) nations. Because of this decision Indian nations were to be treated like any other country by the new nation. Only the government, and not private individuals, could make treaties with Indian nations.

September 17, 1778 ◆ First U.S.-Indian treaty signed

Part of the Delaware tribe signed a peace treaty with the government of the United States. The Delaware Treaty was the first of 370 treaties signed with Indian nations between 1778 and 1871. (In 1871 Congress passed a law forbidding the government to make treaties with Indians.) Between 1778 and 1871 the U.S. Constitution gave the federal government the exclusive power to make treaties with Indian nations. All of these treaties were ratified (approved) by the Senate in the same way treaties with foreign nations were ratified.

Most treaties with the Indians included the following terms:

1) Indians gave up their land in exchange for a reservation.

2) Tribes remained self-governing (sovereign), but under the "protection" of the United States.

3) Indians were given water, hunting, fishing, and gathering rights on reservations, and sometimes on the lands they gave up as well.

4) The federal government would control matters involving non-Indians who were on, or dealing with, reservations. For example, trade between Indians and non-Indians, or crimes involving both, would be under federal control.

5) The United States would give Native nations needed supplies and services, such as food, health care, and education.

Cherokee visitors to London in 1762.

1780s ◆ U.S. settlers moved into the South

In the South, some groups of the Cherokee, Chickasaw, Choctaw, and Creek nations allied themselves with the Spanish in order to try to stop U.S. settler movement into their territories. The Spanish in Florida provided the southern Indians with trade and weapons. Conflict erupted between Native Americans and the U.S. settlers, but most Cherokee, Chickasaw, and Choctaw tried to live peacefully with the settlers. Some antisettler Indians, particularly within the Creek nation and among the Chickamauga Cherokee, remained allied with the Spanish. In the 1790s, however, Spain became involved in wars in Europe and began to ignore its American colonies in the Southeast. The southern Indian nations, now without an ally, were forced to accept the power of the United States.

c. 1780 ◆ Ribbons in Native craftwork

Ribbonwork began to be used among the southern Great Lakes tribes, who decorated their clothing by cutting colorful ribbons of silk and satin into strips and sewing them in intricate patterns on various garments.

THOMAS JEFFERSON ON INDIAN RIGHTS

"It may be regarded as certain, that not a foot of land will ever be taken from the Indians, without their own consent. The sacredness of their rights is felt by all thinking persons in America as much as in Europe."

1783 ◆ Peace of Paris

Under the Peace of Paris, the treaty that ended the American Revolutionary War, the United States received claim to all the land from the Atlantic to the Mississippi River, and from the Great Lakes to the Florida border. Most of these lands, however, belonged to Native Americans.

The British remained in their forts at Detroit and Chicago because the new U.S. government was too weak to force them to leave. The British supplied their Indian allies with goods and weapons, hoping that the Indian nations would prevent the United States from threatening Canada. The Indian nations (Delaware, Miami, Ottawa, Shawnee, and others) hoped the British would help them stop U.S. settlers from taking their land.

1783-84 ◆ Loyalists settled in Canada

American colonists who had remained loyal to the British during the American Revolution were resettled in Canada after the war. These new settlers were given land claimed by the Maliseet, Micmac, and Passamaquoddy tribes along the Atlantic coast north of the United States. These tribes had also been allies of the British during the American Revolutionary War and had been promised this land.

1783-90 ◆ Land sales caused conflict

In order to raise money, the U.S. government claimed all of the Indian land east of the Mississippi River. The new nation sold this land in present-day Indiana, Kentucky, Ohio, and Tennessee. The Chippewa, Delaware, Kickapoo, Miami, Ottawa, Potawatomi, Shawnee, Wyandot, and some Iroquois warriors joined to oppose the invasion of U.S. settlers into their territory. Between 1783 and 1790 perhaps a thousand settlers lost their lives; there are no estimates regarding Indian deaths.

August 7, 1786 ◆ Federal Indian reservations formed

The first federal Indian reservations were established. Congress established northern and southern departments. A superintendent was appointed to lead each

Drawing of the interior of a dwelling at Nootka Sound. Northwest Coast groups lived in large communal houses made of large cedar beams and planks.

department and these officials had the power to grant licenses to trade and live among the Indian people.

1786-95 ◆ Little Turtle's War

Little Turtle of the Miami tribe led an effort with Miami and Shawnee forces to prevent the United States from taking over the area that is now Ohio. In October 1791 Little Turtle defeated a U.S. Army force led by General Arthur St. Clair, governor of the Northwest Territory. U.S. military forces suffered their worst defeat in all of the Indian wars, worse than General Custer's later defeat at the Little Big Horn. President George Washington responded to this defeat by replacing St. Clair with former Revolutionary War hero "Mad" Anthony Wayne. Little Turtle's War ended after the Indian groups were forced to leave this territory because their British allies refused to help them. *(Also see entry dated 1794-95: Battle of Fallen Timbers.)*

1787 ◆ Constitution of the United States

Founders of the United States, such as Benjamin Franklin, Thomas Jefferson, and John Adams, believed that the new U.S. government should be very similar to that of the Iroquois. They wished to use the Five Nations as a model to create a confederacy of states based on unity, democracy, and liberty. Furthermore, the Founding Fathers used Iroquois ideas of individual political freedom, free speech, political equality, and political community. In 1787 Jefferson stated that the "only condition on earth to be compared to [our government] is that of the Indians."

1787 ◆ Northwest Ordinance

In the Northwest Ordinance, the U.S. Congress established the procedure by which territories and states would be created. In order to create new territories and states the U.S. government first had to acquire Indian lands. In the Northwest Ordinance, the United States promised Indians that Native Americans' "land and property shall never be taken from them without their consent; and in their property, rights and liberty, they shall never be invaded or disturbed, unless in just and lawful wars authorized by Congress."

1789 ✦ Europeans contacted Pacific Northwest Indian tribes

The Spanish established a post at Nootka Sound on Vancouver Island. Other European explorers, searching for the Northwest Passage, had come into contact with Indian tribes in the Pacific Northwest (an area stretching north from present-day Oregon to southern Alaska) before, but this was the first permanent European settlement in this area. This was also the first time that the many Native peoples in the area would have to deal with Europeans on an ongoing basis.

There were numerous cultural groups in the area, including the Haida, Tlinglit, and Tsimshian in the north; the Bella Bella, Haihais, Haisla, Kwakiutl, and Owekeeno in present-day British Columbia; the Nootka (or Nuu-Chah-Nulth) on what is now Vancouver Island; the Chinook along the Columbia River; and the Coast Salish tribes of present-day British Columbia, Vancouver Island, and western Washington state. These tribes had striking differences in culture and languages, but they also had many similarities. The typical house in this area was the longhouse. It was large and sheltered several families who were related in some way. Inside the longhouse each family had its own partitioned area. Central fires burned for heat and light, but each family cooked its own meals and ate separately. Families could change houses if they wished.

Salmon was the most abundant and reliable source of food. Although it was the main food source for Northwest Coastal Indians, they also caught many other types of fish, including herring, halibut, and rockfish as well as clams, mussels, and oysters. Marine animals such as porpoise, seals, and whales were also harvested. Land mammals such as bear, deer, elk, and mountain goats were hunted, either by individuals or by groups that would drive them into nets or ambushes. Finally, Northwest Coastal Indians grew and gathered plant foods and berries and fruits.

The potlatch was a central feature of these cultures. A potlatch was a ceremonial feast involving performances and the giving away of valuable gifts. These gifts were given to honor an individual, to strengthen relationships, to display one's generosity, and to honor the memory of those who had passed away.

European traders from England, Russia, Spain, and the United States soon began to fight for control of trade in sea otter pelts. The Native peoples traded these pelts for manufactured goods, which made their work easier and increased their wealth.

1789 ✦ War Department took over Indian affairs

The War Department was created and given control of Indian affairs. Because many Indian nations on the frontier were allied with the British or Spanish and resisted U.S. settlement, the War Department was seen as the best agency to manage Indian relations.

November 19, 1794 ✦ Jay's Treaty

The Treaty of Amity, Commerce, and Navigation between England and the United States (Jay's Treaty) was signed. This treaty reestablished trade between Great Britain and its former colonies. In late 1794 the British agreed to withdraw from fur trade and military posts they occupied in U.S. territory. These posts had been important for maintaining contact between the British and their Indian allies in the United States. With the withdrawal of the English, Indian nations lost an important ally against the United States.

1794-95 ✦ Battle of Fallen Timbers

The Battle of Fallen Timbers, near present-day Fort Wayne, Indiana, took place when bands of Shawnee and Miami led by Little Turtle (Miami), Blue Jacket (Shawnee), and others, went into battle against General Anthony Wayne, known to the Indians as "Blacksnake," in an effort to prevent the takeover of their lands. The Indians were forced to retreat when the British did not support them. *(Also see entry dated 1786-95: Little Turtle's War.)*

1799 ✦ Handsome Lake

Handsome Lake, a Seneca clan leader, became ill and his family and friends gathered to pay their respects before he died. Not long after apparently dying, Handsome Lake recovered and told everyone that his soul left his body and went outside, where he met three Native angels. The angels told Handsome Lake that he should quit drinking, live a good life, and follow the teachings of the Creator, who would reveal himself in the months ahead.

In the fall of 1799 Handsome Lake had another vision and, speaking an ancient form of the Iroquois language, called his people to return to traditional ways. Handsome Lake condemned drinking, violence, and sexual promiscuity as enemies of Native American family life. He stressed traditional values and the need for the well-being of the whole society. Handsome Lake taught the Iroquois to tolerate American culture, but with caution. His visions and teachings were known as the *Gaiwiio*—the good word. Handsome Lake died in 1815, but his Iroquois followers kept his teachings alive. One result of Handsome Lake's work was the establishment of the Longhouse religion, a uniquely Iroquois faith and practice. By the late 1830s the religion became the Handsome Lake church.

1803 • Louisiana Purchase

The United States bought from France a large portion of land west of the Mississippi River extending in the north to the Pacific Ocean for $15 million. (This territory today makes up the states of Arkansas, Iowa, Kansas, Louisiana, Missouri, Montana, Nebraska, North Dakota, Oklahoma, and South Dakota and parts of Colorado, Minnesota, and Wyoming.) This land contained large numbers of Indian nations, many of whom had not had contact with European or U.S. governments. President Thomas Jefferson proposed that many of the Indian nations living east of the Mississippi River be removed west to lands where they would be out of the way of U.S. settlers, and the eastern land would be open to settlement.

1805-06 • Sacajawea helped expedition

While explorers William Clark and Meriwether Lewis were on an expedition that took them from St. Louis, Missouri, to the Pacific Ocean, they met Sacajawea in present-day North Dakota. Sacajawea was a Shoshoni woman married to a French trader, Toussaint Charbonneau. Sacajawea and her husband joined Lewis and Clark's expedition, and Sacajawea proved invaluable to the success of the undertaking. She spoke several Indian languages, and the presence of a woman was seen as a peaceful sign by other tribes. During the journey Sacajawea revealed to Lewis and Clark important passageways through the wilderness and also provided the expedition with valuable information about edible plants.

Lewis and Clark came into contact in their travels with several Indian tribes, including the Cayuse, Nez Percé, Walla Walla, Wishram, and Yakima. Relations between the explorers and Native peoples were friendly. They traded goods, and Lewis and Clark honored some of the chiefs with medals bearing the words "peace" and "friendship."

Upon their return, Lewis and Clark reported the many wondrous things they had seen, including vast numbers of fur-bearing animals. The United States claimed the entire Northwest as their territory, and encouraged settlers to relocate to the region. *(Also see entry dated 1810: Fur trading in the Great Basin.)*

HOW FAIR WERE TREATIES?

Starting in the late 1700s and continuing through the early 1900s, the U.S. government bought over 20 million square miles of Indian land. Most of these purchases were made through treaties and agreements negotiated with tribal groups. The American public remained, for the most part, unconcerned about the fairness of the way lands were passing from Native Americans to the government, and many "sales" were forced upon the tribes.

Although the Indians had a long history of signing treaties among themselves, they had never before considered giving away or selling their land. Territory was owned by a particular nation or shared with neighbors, but it was never given away, and only lost through war. Many American Indian tribes did not believe they were giving away all rights to their lands. Often when they signed treaties, they felt they were merely agreeing to share their territory.

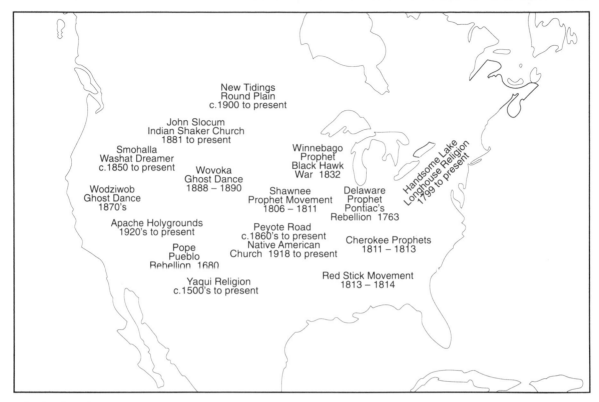

Native American
revitalization
movements.

1806-09 ✦ Tecumseh and Tenskwatawa, the Shawnee Prophet

In February 1806, while living among the Delaware and Munsee in the pre-sent-day Munsee, Indiana, area, a Shawnee man named Tenskwatawa reportedly died. While his family prepared him for burial, he regained consciousness, say-ing that he had died and visited the Master of Life. Tenskwatawa told his peo-ple that through him, The Open Door, Native Americans could learn "The Way." Tenskwatawa became known as the "Shawnee Prophet."

Thousands of Indians became followers of Tenskwatawa and his teachings and traveled to hear him preach in a village called Prophetstown. Tenskwatawa urged his people not to sell Indian land, to reject European ways, and to renew Indian traditions. In particular Tenskwatawa warned against the use of alcohol, which was devastating many Indian communities. Through his teachings Ten-skwatawa united many tribes to oppose the United States. Tenskwatawa's brother, Tecumseh (whose name means "Goes Through One Place to Another"), used these teachings to create a military and political confederacy of Indian tribes. Tecumseh learned about warfare early in his life. In his early teens he took part in the American Revolution on the side of the British. Tecumseh, Ten-skwatawa, and their followers rejected treaties with the United States, claiming that all the land belonged to all Indians. "Sell a country! Why not sell the air, the great sea, as well as the earth? Did not the Great Spirit make them all for the use of his children?" Tecumseh asked, responding to news of a treaty selling Indian land. *(Also see entry dated 1811: Battle of Tippecanoe.)*

April 6, 1808 ◆ *The Indian Princess* produced
The Indian Princess was the first play written about an American Indian. It was produced on April 6, 1808, at the Chestnut Theatre in Philadelphia, Pennsylvania.

1810 ◆ Fur trading in the Great Basin
British traders traveled through the area explored by Lewis and Clark, and soon three major fur trading companies set up trading posts or factories in the Northwest. These were the Northwest Company, the American Fur Company, and the Hudson's Bay Company. The traders were eager to take advantage of the furs and horses provided by the Indians. *(Also see entry dated 1805-06: Sacajawea helped expedition.)*

1811 ◆ Battle of Tippecanoe
Governor William Henry Harrison of Indiana (the future U.S. president) attacked Prophetstown with 1,000 soldiers. Tenskwatawa told his followers that his spiritual power would protect them from army bullets, but the Indians suffered significant casualties in the battle. As a result of the Battle of Tippecanoe, the Indian confederacy was weakened, and the Shawnee Prophet lost most of his power as his followers abandoned him. Tecumseh joined the British to fight against the Americans in the War of 1812 and was killed at the Battle of the Thames on October 5, 1813. *(Also see entry dated 1806-09: Tecumseh and Tenskwatawa, the Shawnee Prophet.)*

1812-15 ◆ War of 1812
The War of 1812, fought between the United States and Great Britain, devastated the land and populations of the Indians of the Old Northwest. In the Treaty of Ghent, which ended the war, the British agreed that all the territory south of the Great Lakes belonged to the United States. The British also agreed not to give any help to their Indian allies in this territory. This left the Indian nations living east of the Mississippi River entirely under the control of the U.S. government. Native Americans no longer had the supplies to help them fight against the United States.

1813-14 ◆ Red Stick War
Influenced by Tecumseh's message of resistance to the United States, some groups of Creek called Red Stick, who lived primarily in present-day Alabama, attacked the villages of other groups of Creek who were allied with the United

States. The Red Stick also attacked Fort Mims, killing most of the U.S. citizens there, which brought the United States into the Creek civil war. General Andrew Jackson (the future U.S. president) attacked the Red Stick village of Tohopeka at Horseshoe Bend on the Tallapoosa River in Alabama. Surrounded and assaulted by cannon, the Creek suffered losses of more than 800 men, women, and children. With the end of resistance of the Red Stick, the Creek Nation was forced to give much of its land in Alabama and Georgia—22 million acres in all—to the United States. *(Also see entry dated 1806-09: Tecumseh and Tenskwatawa, the Shawnee Prophet; and 1836: Creek removal.)*

1815–1830s ◆ Indian migrations

Many Indian groups from the North and East moved into Texas to escape from the United States. These were groups from the Cherokee, Delaware, Kickapoo, and Shawnee nations. Together these groups formed a loose union and developed a comfortable alliance with the Mexican rulers of Texas. Their lives changed for the worse when Texas gained its independence in the 1830s.

June 19, 1816 ◆ Battle of Seven Oaks

A group of Métis killed 21 residents of the Hudson's Bay Company's Red River Colony, near present-day Winnipeg, Manitoba, in the Battle of Seven Oaks. This battle was important in promoting a sense of nationhood among the Métis.

The Métis eventually settled around the Red River Colony. There they were employed in small-scale farming, buffalo hunting, and seasonal employment in the fur trade where Métis acted as guides, interpreters, and boatmen. Their sense of separate identity was strengthened by their annual buffalo hunts, their unique Métchif language derived from European and Indian languages, and their own folklore, music, dances, and flag. They developed a unique two-wheeled cart, called the Red River cart, to carry their possessions and provisions.

1817-18 ◆ First Seminole War

Some Red Stick joined the Seminole in Florida and continued resistance to the United States with the help of English trade companies. U.S. forces led by General Andrew Jackson destroyed Seminole villages and farms in northern Florida. These attacks led Spain to sell Florida to the United States. *(Also see entry dated 1835-42: Second Seminole War.)*

1817-19 ◆ Cherokee migration

Several thousand Cherokee moved beyond the Mississippi into Arkansas, forming a Cherokee Nation West, because of continuing conflict with U.S. settlers. These early Cherokee migrants later become known as Old Settlers, since they were the first Cherokee to settle in Arkansas and to migrate, in the late 1820s, to Indian Territory (Oklahoma).

Métis warriors win victory over Red River colonists at a shootout at Seven Oaks.

1819 ◆ Spanish sold Florida and West Florida

Spain sold Florida and West Florida, containing parts of the present-day states of Alabama and Mississippi, to the U.S. government. The United States now controlled all land east of the Mississippi River.

1821 ◆ Mexico declared its independence

Mexico gained its independence from Spain. This meant that Native Americans living in what are now the states of Arizona, California, and New Mexico would have new rulers. The Mexican Constitution of 1824 guaranteed equality of citizenship to all under Mexican rule, including California's Indian peoples. Only the Pueblo, however, were ever given Mexican citizenship.

1823 ◆ Cherokee Syllabary

Sequoyah, a Cherokee who did not have formal education or knowledge of English, developed the Cherokee syllabary—a system of writing that uses characters (letters) to represent whole syllables—after deciding that his language should have its own writing system. His writing code used symbols for the sounds of syllables (a combination of a vowel and a consonant) rather than for sounds of each individual letter, as in an alphabet. Although members of his tribe were fearful of his work, thinking Sequoyah was practicing witchcraft, many Cherokee quickly learned to read and write with the Cherokee syllabary. The Bible was translated into Cherokee, and Cherokee spiritual leaders and healers recorded sacred and medicinal knowledge.

1823 ✦ *Johnson* v. *McIntosh*

In *Johnson* v. *McIntosh*, a case tried before the U.S. Supreme Court, Chief Justice John Marshall stated that Indians had the right to use land in areas conquered by the United States, but that the land belonged to the federal government. Native Americans could use this land, but they could sell it only to the U.S. government. This hurt the Native American tribes because it limited their control over the use and sale of their own territory.

1823 ✦ *Poor Sarah*

This fictional account of an Indian girl's religious conversion is considered the first work of American Indian fiction. *Poor Sarah* was written by Elias Boudinot, a Cherokee who later became editor of the *Cherokee Phoenix,* a tribal newspaper, in the late 1820s.

1824 ✦ Native resistance to Spanish missions

The Native peoples of California, forced to work as slaves on Spanish missions, found many ways to resist their masters. Workers refused to learn Spanish, or pretended they could not understand commands given in Spanish. They would do their work slowly and poorly.

Some Native American women who were sexually assaulted and impregnated by Spanish soldiers practiced abortion or infanticide (killing the newborn baby). They did not want to give birth to children of the enemy, thereby providing a new generation of slave labor for the colonists. Secret religious activities arose, and Native American people tried to keep their traditional beliefs alive. Running away was another alternative, but this was made difficult by soldiers patrolling the area around the missions.

Mission uprisings also occurred. In 1834 Indians from three missions arose to protect their lives and regain their lost freedom. After taking over one mission for more than a month, most were persuaded to surrender after a cannon assault by Spanish troops. However, a number refused to return to the missions. They issued this defiant message to authorities who demanded their return: "We shall maintain ourselves with what God will provide for us in the open country. Moreover, we are soldiers, stone-masons, carpenters, etc., and we will provide for ourselves by our work." *(Also see entries dated 1769: First mission established in California; and 1836: Mission system in California collapsed.)*

1827 ◆ *Ancient History of the Six Nations*
Considered to be the first historical work by an American Indian author, the *Ancient History of the Six Nations* was published by David Cusick, a Tuscarora Indian.

1827-28 ◆ Cherokee Republic
The Cherokee, in an attempt to prevent the U.S. government from forcing them off their land, formed the Cherokee Republic. The Cherokee established a capital in New Echota, in present-day Georgia. In 1827 they wrote a constitution that called for three branches of government, in many ways similar to the U.S. Constitution. In 1828 the Cherokee elected John Ross, a wealthy Cherokee slaveholder, as their principal chief. The Cherokee hoped that their new government would be able to preserve their homeland in present-day Georgia, Tennessee, and eastern Alabama. The Georgia state legislature, wanting to move the Cherokee off their lands, passed a series of laws that abolished the Cherokee government and took their territory. *(Also see entry dated May 1838-March 1839: "Trail of Tears.")*

1828-35 ◆ *The Cherokee Phoenix*
The *Cherokee Phoenix*, a weekly newspaper printed in English and in the Cherokee syllabary, was published and widely read. During these years, the Cherokee people had a higher literacy rate (the percentage of people who could read and write) than the settlers who lived nearby. *(Also see entries dated 1823: Cherokee Syllabary; and 1835: Cherokee Phoenix closed down.)*

1829 ◆ Last Beothuk died
Shanawdithit, the last of the Beothuk, died. The Beothuk, who lived on the present-day island of Newfoundland, had been devastated by warfare and epidemic diseases and were now extinct as a people.

July 1829 ◆ Gold discovered on Cherokee land
Gold was discovered on Cherokee land. The gold seekers arrived in overwhelming numbers and lawlessness began. Georgia increased its efforts to relocate the Cherokee to lands west of the Mississippi River.

ALEXIS DE TOQUEVILLE ON INDIAN REMOVAL

After visiting the United States, Alexis de Toqueville, French nobleman and political scientist, wrote, "They [the U.S. government] kindly take the Indian by the hand and lead them to a grave far from the lands of their fathers.... It is impossible to destroy mankind with more respect for the laws of humanity." De Toqueville predicted that Indians would be "driven from one 'final' location to another until their only refuge is the grave."

PRESIDENT ANDREW JACKSON ADDRESSED INDIAN REMOVAL

President Andrew Jackson, in his second annual message, addressed the question of the removal of the eastern Indian tribes to the west of the Mississippi River. "Philanthropy could not wish to see this continent restored to the condition in which it was found by our forefathers. What good man would prefer a country covered with forests and ranged by a few thousand savages to our extensive Republic, studded with cities, towns, and prosperous farms, embellished with all the improvements which art can devise or industry execute, occupied by more than 12 million happy people, and filled with all the blessings of liberty, civilization and religion? The present policy of the Government is but a continuation of the same progressive change by a milder process."

April 13, 1830 ✦ Canadian reserves

Upper Canada established a system of reserves (the Canadian term for what are called reservations in the United States) for its Indians. The changes of 1830 marked the beginning of a policy aimed at assimilating (the process whereby a minority group gradually adopts the customs and attitudes of a dominant culture) Indians into non–Native society.

c. 1830-50 ✦ Beadwork on the Plains

Distinctive styles of beadwork embroidery emerged across the Great Plains, largely replacing the more time-consuming traditional quillwork forms. Beadwork designs decorated shirts, dresses, leggings, cradleboards, knife cases, gun cases, tobacco and medicine bags, and many other objects.

1830-60 ✦ Removal period

On May 28, 1830, the U.S. Congress voted in favor of the Indian Removal Act. The removal of Native Americans from their lands in the east to Indian Territory (present-day Oklahoma) became an important part of national Indian policy. During the 1830s and 1840s the U.S. Army forced thousands of Indian families to leave their belongings and move to lands west of present-day Iowa, Missouri, Kansas, Nebraska, Arkansas, and Oklahoma. Southern tribes to be removed included the Cherokee, Chickasaw, Choctaw, Creek, Seminole, and parts of other groups. In the North, the Delaware, Miami, Ottawa, Peoria, Potawatomi, Sauk and Fox, Seneca, and Wyandot tribes were removed. The government was not prepared to provide supplies for so many Indians along the trails and in new homes, causing great suffering and death for the Native Americans. In 1841, Major Ethan Allan Hitchcock investigated Indian affairs in the West and concluded that the American Indian policy was filled with "bribery, perjury and forgery, short weights, issues of spoiled meat and grain, and every conceivable subterfuge [trick]."

1831 ✦ *Cherokee Nation* v. *Georgia*

When the state of Georgia tried to remove the Cherokee from their homeland, the Cherokee took the case to the U.S. Supreme Court. They based their case on a clause in the Constitution that allowed foreign nations to seek redress (compensation or remedy) in the Supreme Court for damages caused by U.S. citizens.

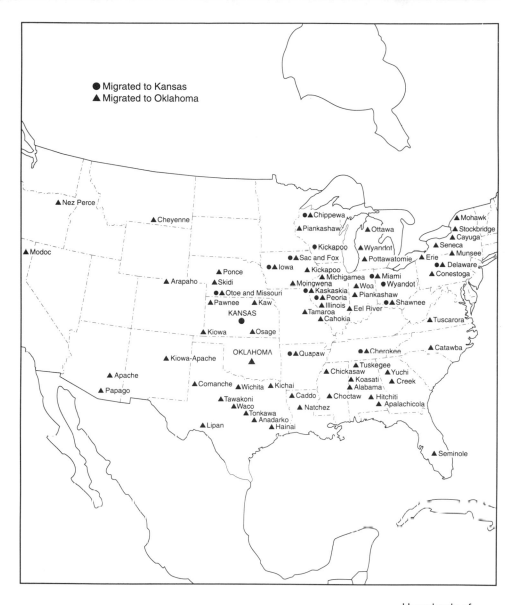

Homelands of
Indian nations
forced to migrate
after 1830 to
Indian Territory.

The court ruled that Indian nations were not foreign nations, but dependent, domestic nations. Up until that time, U.S. law had treated Indian nations as separate, or foreign, nations. The court ruled, therefore, that the Cherokee could not sue. *(Also see entries dated 1827-28:* Cherokee Republic*; 1832:* Worcester v. Georgia*; 1835:* Cherokee Phoenix *closed down; and May 1838-March 1839: "Trail of Tears.")*

Artist George Catlin portrayed the Choctaws playing games after observing them for hours in their new "home" in Indian Territory.

1831-39 ✦ George Catlin painted the Plains

Artist George Catlin traveled through the West and created an "Indian Gallery" of portraits. In the approximately seven years of his project, Catlin traveled by horse and canoe throughout the Plains, from eastern Texas to Montana, documenting the many Indian nations he encountered. He also journeyed to the Gulf states and the Southeast. During this time Catlin encountered Arikara, Assiniboine, Blackfoot, Hidatsa, Iowa, Mandan, Miccosukee, Missouri, Omaha, Oto, Pawnee, Sauk and Fox, Seminole, and different Sioux groups. During his life Catlin painted numerous important Indian leaders, including Osceola, the Seminole resistance leader; Black Hawk and Keokuk of the Sauk (Sac) and Fox; Tenskwatawa (Tecumseh's brother, the Shawnee Prophet); and many other Native men and women. Additionally, Catlin portrayed ceremonies and lifeways of the numerous cultures he observed. Since his paintings documented an era for which no comparably extensive record exists, Catlin's observations and works are an important source of information about American Indian peoples, particularly about the height of the Great Plains culture.

1832 ✦ Black Hawk War

Black Hawk, chief of the Sauk (Sac) and Fox, returned from a winter hunting trip to find that his village had been invaded by U.S. settlers. He asked them to leave, but they refused. Black Hawk was strongly opposed to giving up any Sauk and Fox land in Illinois and Wisconsin. When he and his followers returned to plant a crop on their former lands the next year, they were driven from the land by Illinois militia and U.S. troops. Both Abraham Lincoln and Jefferson Davis (future president of the Confederate States of America) were members of the force that ultimately defeated Black Hawk and massacred many of his followers, attacking them even after they tried to surrender. The Sauk and Fox were forced to promise never to return, live, fish, or plant on their previous homelands.

1832 ◆ *Worcester* v. *Georgia*

In *Worcester* v. *Georgia* the U.S. Supreme Court ruled that Georgia could not remove the Cherokee from their land, stating that only the federal government had the right to regulate Indian affairs; states could not extend their laws over Indian governments such as the Cherokee Republic. Chief Justice John Marshall declared in the Court's decision: "The Cherokee Nation is a distinct community occupying its own territory in which the laws of Georgia can have no effect and which the citizens of Georgia have no right to enter, but with the assent of the Cherokees themselves." Despite this ruling, the Cherokee were still forced to move to Indian Territory. (*Also see entries dated 1827-28: Cherokee Republic; 1831: Cherokee Nation v. Georgia; 1835: Cherokee Phoenix closed down; and May 1838-March 1839: "Trail of Tears."*)

1833 ◆ Kenekuk, the Kickapoo Prophet

The Kickapoo, a tribe that lived in present-day Illinois, were removed to what is now Kansas. Kenekuk, the religious and political leader of the Kickapoo, claimed he had a vision from the Great Spirit for the Indian people. Kenekuk's vision was different from that of the Shawnee Prophet before him in that he was told that the Kickapoo should accept U.S. culture and land demands. The Kickapoo Prophet worked to create a new moral and religious community for his followers, one that included Catholic, Protestant, and traditional Kickapoo religious beliefs. He also encouraged his people to take up agriculture (farming) and to form self-sufficient Indian farming communities. The Kickapoo Prophet banned alcohol and instructed his followers to maintain friendly relations with U.S. settlers in order to preserve their lands. Kenekuk died in 1852, but his community survives until this day, and the people retain the distinct religious teachings of the Kickapoo Prophet.

1835 ◆ *Cherokee Phoenix* closed down

The Cherokee newspaper, the *Cherokee Phoenix,* was denied freedom of the press as guaranteed by the first amendment of the U.S. Constitution when the Georgia governor decided to close down the paper for opposing his policies. (*Also see entry dated 1828-35: The Cherokee Phoenix.*)

Osceola, the
Black Drink, a
Seminole warrior.

December 29, 1835 ◆ Treaty of New Echota

In the Treaty of New Echota (the capitol of the Cherokee Republic) a small group of Cherokee, the Treaty Party, sold all remaining Cherokee land east of the Mississippi River to the United States. The majority of the Cherokee opposed the treaty. The Treaty of New Echota led to Cherokee removal and the "Trail of Tears." *(Also see entry dated May 1838-March 1839: "Trail of Tears.")*

1835-42 ◆ Second Seminole War

In the winter of 1835, after the Seminole refused to leave their land in Florida, they were led by war chief Osceola in a fight against U.S. army troops in the swamps of Florida. The war would cost the U.S. government more than $20 million and the lives of 1,500 troops. Osceola was captured during a truce and died in prison in 1838. The war continued until 1842, at which time most Seminole were moved west of the Mississippi River. *(Also see entry dated 1817-18: First Seminole War.)*

1836 ◆ Creek removal

The condition of the Creek in Alabama worsened. U.S. settlers moved in on Creek land and purchased all available food so that the Creek were unable to buy even corn or meat. Drought and famine combined to increase Creek difficulties. Facing disaster, the Creek realized they would have to move and agreed to go to Indian Territory. *(Also see entry dated 1813-14: Red Stick War.)*

1836 ◆ Mission system in California collapsed

The mission system in California finally collapsed. Devastating epidemics and slave labor were responsible for killing the majority of Native California people who came into contact with the Spanish colonists.

Native Americans left the missions to find that their former land had been changed forever. Animals and crops introduced to the area by the Spanish made it virtually impossible for California Indians to live off the land in the way they had before the Spanish came. Some tribes and villages had disappeared. *(Also see entry dated 1824: Native Resistance to Spanish missions.)*

May 1838-March 1839 ◆ "Trail of Tears"

Removal of the Cherokee began when General Winfield Scott and 7,000 federal troops were sent to complete the removal of the Cherokee from the state of Geor-

Painting of the Cherokee Trail of Tears.

gia. The U.S. government said the Cherokee would be sent to Indian Territory (present-day Oklahoma), where "they can establish and enjoy a government of their choice and perpetuate such a state of society as may be most consonant with their views, habits and conditions." Scott's troops forcibly rounded up the Cherokee and placed them in stockades in preparation for starting them on the long trail to Indian Territory. The U.S. government imprisoned any Cherokee who refused to abandon their lands, and burned their homes and crops. The Cherokee remember the trek as "The Trail Where They Cried," while U.S. historians call it "The Trail of Tears." The difficult march began in October 1838; it cost the Cherokee one–fourth of their population, or more than 4,000 men, women, and children. One soldier wrote: "I fought through the Civil War and have seen men shot to pieces and slaughtered by thousands, but the Cherokee removal was the cruelest work I ever knew."

The survivors reached their destination in late March 1839, reorganized themselves in the new area and prospering despite the odds, retaining their language and alphabet to the present day. The move involved 16,000 persons and was only the first of many trails of tears for the eastern and southern Indian nations. *(Also see entries dated 1827-28: Cherokee Republic; 1831: Cherokee Nation v. Georgia: 1832: Worcester v. Georgia; and December 29, 1835: Treaty of New Echota.)*

1840-60 ◆ Indian Territory and the Indian State

During the 1840s and 1850s U.S. officials followed a plan of moving all Indians to Indian Territory, in what is now Kansas and Oklahoma. By doing so, U.S. officials believed that more land could be opened to settlers, and the Indians could enter the United States with their own state. This plan did not work, however, since U.S. settlers continued to take Indian lands, and the Indian state was never established. Many Indian groups did not want to move to Indian Territory, and most did not want to be included in the U.S. Congress or government.

1840–90 ◆ Golden Age of Northwest Coastal Art

With improved tools and greater wealth brought by the fur trade, the art of the Northwest coast flourished during the mid-nineteenth century. Among the arts of the region were dancing blankets, weavings, button blankets, and a variety of sculptural forms, including ceremonial masks, rattles, and the well-known totem poles.

January 26, 1841 ◆ Micmac appealed to Queen Victoria

Queen Victoria of England received an appeal from the Micmac of present-day Nova Scotia regarding the loss of hunting grounds and the taking of lands the Micmac claimed as their own. The population of the Micmac at this time was declining steadily. Queen Victoria's interest prompted an investigation.

Joseph Howe was appointed as an unpaid Indian commissioner. He was authorized to prevent non–Natives from settling on Micmac lands, to see that money was spent to help Indians adjust to a different life-style, and to provide for Indian education. Despite this mission the government was unable to prevent settlers from taking Micmac land. *(Also see entries dated 1713: Micmac resisted the English; and November 22, 1752: Halifax Treaty.)*

1843 ◆ Eskimo Mission School

The Russian-Greek Orthodox church established the first mission school for the Inuit (Eskimos) in Nushagak, Alaska.

1843 ◆ Oregon Trail

The Oregon Trail was opened from Idaho across Oregon to the Grande Ronde Valley. Soon many settlers used the Oregon Trail to travel to the Pacific Northwest Coast. The newcomers established territorial governments in present-day Washington and Oregon and asserted political power over the Native peoples.

Diseases brought by the settlers spread rapidly among the Indians, killing many. Tensions and conflict mounted. Soon after, the Gold Rush spread north from California into the plateau and mountains, and miners invaded. The gold miners showed little or no regard for the rights of the Indians.

1843 ◆ Wampum belts

During an important tribal council meeting at Tahlequah, in present-day Oklahoma, Cherokee members made wampum belts to depict the peace they had concluded with the Iroquois prior to the Revolutionary War.

1844 ◆ *Report on the Affairs of the Indians of Canada*

The Canadian Commission on Indian Affairs (the Bagot Commission) issued its *Report on the Affairs of the Indians of Canada*. Describing the conditions among Canada's Indians (particularly in Upper Canada) as terrible, it criticized the lack of a consistent Indian policy in the Province of Canada (formerly Upper Canada and Lower Canada). It recommended that Indian land rights be recognized and the efforts to assimilate (to coerce to become like the dominant society) Indians continued. These dual recommendations of protection and assimilation became the basis of Canadian Indian policy for over a century.

1844-45 ◆ U.S. military posts were built

The U.S. Congress passed laws to build military posts to protect settlers moving from the East to California and Oregon. These forts caused conflict with Indian tribes along the route.

1846 ◆ Annexation of Texas

With the annexation (the adding of territory to an existing country) of Texas by the United States, additional Indian tribes were placed under U.S. governmental control. By the terms of a general peace treaty the Caddo, Comanche, Lipan, Kichai, and Wichita Indians recognized the authority of the U.S. government.

1846 ◆ Navajo resistance

At the end of the Mexican-American War, U.S. settlers moved into California and New Mexico, where the *Diné* (Navajo for "the people," which they called themselves) faced the U.S. Army. The Navajo were one of the first Indian nations in the American Southwest to deal with the government of the United States. Between 1600 and 1846 the Navajo had confronted the *Nakai,* or Spanish. Once the Europeans had introduced cattle, sheep, and horses to the Native peoples in the area, the Navajo had built up large herds of these animals by raiding the Spanish and other tribes.

The Navajo continued to raid U.S. settlements in present-day New Mexico, leading to conflict with the U.S. Army. Many Navajo cornfields were burned, fruit

A sketch of Fort Laramie, in Wyoming, the site of major treaties with the northern Plains Indians in 1851 and 1868.

trees were destroyed, sheep were slaughtered, and communities were ruined. The Navajo successfully resisted for 17 years. But, facing starvation in 1863 and 1864, they finally surrendered. *(Also see entry dated 1864: Long Walk of the Navajo.)*

1846-48 ◆ Mexican–American War

As a result of the Treaty of Guadalupe-Hildalgo, which ended the Mexican-American War, the United States took control of the territory that now makes up the states of Arizona, California, Nevada, New Mexico, and Utah and parts of present-day Colorado and Wyoming. Nations such as the Kiowa, Modoc, Navajo, and Sioux fought against the U.S. Army in an attempt to prevent the U.S. government from taking their land. Others tribes such as the Blackfeet, Caddo, Crow, Hopi, and Nespelem did not fight. Whether the tribes fought or not, their fate was the same. Their lands were taken either through treaties or conquest. Many Indians were relocated to lands controlled by their neighbors. Others were concentrated on reservations with other Indian nations, including former enemies.

1847 ◆ Pueblo revolt

The Taos Pueblo Indians, angered by the conduct of the United States during the Mexican War, attacked and killed the U.S. governor of New Mexico. U.S. troops retaliated by attacking Taos Pueblo and killing approximately 165 Indians.

1848 ◆ California Gold Rush

Gold was discovered at Sutter's Mill in California. At first Native Americans in California worked in the gold mines, contributing significantly to their discovery and success. Soon, however, settlers flooded into California hoping to become rich. Widespread abuse and murder of Indian men, women, and children took place as miners saw them as competitors in the gold field and barriers to the opening of additional land for gold exploration. The discovery of gold meant the beginning of the end for many of the California Indian tribes. *(Also see entry dated 1851: Reservations in California.)*

Mid-1850s ◆ Cheyenne migrate to Plains

By this time the Cheyenne had moved to the western Plains and had fully adopted the Plains culture. They practiced the Sun Dance ceremony, had military societies of young men, and lived in portable tepees. In the summer they gathered to celebrate religious ceremonies; in the winter the Cheyenne (like the Blackfeet, Crow, Sioux, and other Plains nations) broke up into small bands and spent the cold winter months in separate locations.

With so many new Indian nations moving into the area, the Indian peoples who were originally from the Plains considered the newcomers hostile intruders. The original Plains Indians, like the Pawnee and Ponca, tried to defend their traditional hunting territories. The newly arrived eastern Indians tried to re-create their communities in the Plains territory. It was no surprise that conflict resulted. *(Also see entry dated c. 1770: Horses lead to development of High Plains Culture.)*

1850 ◆ Smohalla and the Indian Shaker church

Many Indian peoples of the Northwest Plateau (present-day western Washington) joined a new religious movement, *Waptashi,* or the Feather Religion. The religion was founded on the teachings of Smohalla, the Wanapum prophet, who was said to have died on two occasions and traveled to the Sky World. There the Creator revealed to Smohalla the sacred dance and ceremony known as the Washat and told him to return to his people and to remember the ceremonies of thanks for first foods and other gifts of creation. Smohalla led a fierce resistance to selling land and provided a new belief that mixed both Christian and traditional northwestern Indian ideas.

The new religion helped individual Indians and Indian communities better cope with the rapidly changing conditions of their lives. Smohalla's church later

Captain Jack, a
Modoc leader.

became known as the Indian Shaker Church and continued to gather followers among several northwestern Indian nations such as the Nez Percé. (The Shakers were members of a religious movement begun in England in the mid-1700s. Shakers lived in communes and practiced self-denial and strict spiritual discipline.)

1851 ◆ Reservations in California

Early reservations were created in California on military reserves to protect the Native population from the violence of U.S. citizens. In reality the government reserves served fewer than 2,000 Indians at any given time. The vast majority of California Indians survived as best they could on their own. They withdrew into remote areas in their attempt to avoid contact with settlers, but violence against them continued. Casual murder of individuals, vigilante raids, and even occasional army massacres took place. Governor Burnett told the state legislature that a "war of extermination will continue to be waged between the races until the Indian race becomes extinct" and that it was "beyond the power and wisdom of man" to avert the "inevitable destiny of this [the Indian] race."

Some Indian groups continued to fight. The last and largest war against the California Indians was fought against the Modoc Indians. Under the leadership of Captain Jack, 50 Modoc warriors and their families held off an army of over 3,000 for nearly a year. In the end, Captain Jack and three others surrendered and were hanged. Captain Jack and Schochin John were decapitated (had their heads cut off) following their deaths, and their heads eventually wound up in the Smithsonian Institution in Washington, D.C. *(Also see entry dated 1848: California Gold Rush.)*

1853 ◆ Gadsden Purchase

The Gadsden Purchase, an agreement between the United States and Mexico, brought to the United States portions of the states of Arizona, California, and New Mexico and set the present U.S. border with Mexico. The purchase brought many Indian nations in these future states under U.S. jurisdiction.

1853 ◆ Oregon and Washington territories formed

The United States created the Oregon Territory and the Washington Territory. U.S. policy in the area toward Indians was focused on taking title to their lands, moving Indians onto reservations, and establishing military and civil power over the tribes.

Gold was discovered in Oregon Territory in the mid-1800s. The U.S. Army responded to violence between miners and the Yakima Indians by sending troops, who invaded the lands of the Walla Walla, Umatilla, Cayuse, and Palouse Indians. The resulting Plateau Indian War brought the full powers of the government on many Plateau groups. Few of these groups had been involved in the conflict, but the volunteer soldiers sought to punish all Indians.

U.S. settlers' contact with Great Basin peoples came relatively late in the 1850s. Many of these peoples, who had lived by hunting animals and gathering roots and plants, went to work for U.S. ranchers and farmers. Some worked as cowboys driving cattle. Others worked at such jobs as planting, cultivating, and harvesting grains, or taking care of livestock.

1853-56 ◆ Indian treaties

During this period 52 treaties were signed with Indian nations resulting in the purchase of 174 million acres of Indian land by the U.S. government. The Indian nations that signed these treaties were forced to accept small pieces of land commonly called "reservations." In some cases Indians kept the right to hunt and fish on their former lands, but these rights were often ignored. *(Also see entry dated 1871: Canadian "numbered treaties.")*

1854 ◆ *Life and Adventures of Joaquin Murieta* published

The first American Indian novel, *Life and Adventures of Joaquin Murieta,* was written by John Rollins Ridge, a Cherokee. Ridge moved to California after his tribe was removed to Oklahoma during the 1830s. His father and brother were murdered because they favored removal. Ridge became a newspaperman and eventually owner of his own newspaper. In his novel, the hero is an outlaw with a heart, who avenges the downtrodden as he goes from one wild adventure to another.

1855-65 ◆ Five Civilized Tribes formed governments

Between 1855 and 1865 the Cherokee, Chickasaw, Choctaw, Seminole and Creek formed new governments in Indian Territory (present-day Oklahoma). Each of these governments was made up of an executive, legislative, and judicial system, much like the U.S. government. Each tribe was ruled by its own government until Oklahoma became a state in 1907. The Five Civilized Tribes were so named by non-Native observers because of their governments and their exceptional education programs.

1857 ◆ Gradual Civilization Act in Canada

The Imperial (British) Government passed the Gradual Civilization Act, which made Canadian Indians noncitizens but created a process by which Indians could

WESTWARD EXPANSION

POPULATION FRONTIERS TO 1860

LAND CESSIONS TO 1859

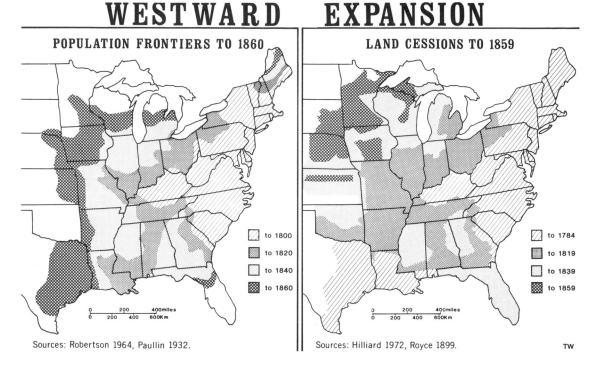

to 1800
to 1820
to 1840
to 1860

to 1784
to 1819
to 1839
to 1859

Sources: Robertson 1964, Paullin 1932.

Sources: Hilliard 1972, Royce 1899.

TW

Westward
expansion until
the 1860s.

become citizens. Indian males seeking enfranchisement—the acceptance of Canadian citizenship and the giving up of any legal distinction as an Indian—would need to demonstrate that they were educated, debt free, capable of managing their own affairs, and of "good moral character." Enfranchised individuals would be granted their share of band (tribal) funds and ownership of land. In order to acquaint unenfranchised Indians with the Canadian political system, the act encouraged the formation of elected band councils (to replace traditional leaders) by offering such councils limited powers over reserve (the Canadian term for reservation) affairs. Most Indian bands opposed these nontraditional governments. *(Also see entry dated 1869: Gradual Enfranchisement Act.)*

1861 ◆ Reservations in New Mexico

General James Carleton of the U.S. Army formed Indian reservations in New Mexico. Carleton planned to gather Apache and Navajo together "little by little onto a Reservation away from the haunts and hills and hiding places of their own county, and there be kind to them: there teach their children how to read and write; teach them the art of peace; teach them the truths of Christianity." Carleton represented reformers who wanted to place Indians on reservations where they would "acquire new habits, new ideas, new modes of life: the old Indians will die off ... the young ones will take their places ... and thus, little by little, they will become a happy and contented people."

Despite Carleton's stated intentions to gently assimilate Native peoples to U.S. culture, he killed many Indians while trying to force them onto reservations. The U.S. Army burned Navajo cornfields, destroyed fruit trees, slaughtered sheep, and ruined communities. Christopher (Kit) Carson, a New Mexico trader, was made a colonel in the U.S. Army. During the 1860s he led an army of volunteers to capture and settle first the Apache and then numerous Navajo bands.

1862-64 ◆ Little Crow's Uprising
The Santee Sioux, led by Little Crow, revolted against corrupt Indian agents in Minnesota who refused to provide Indians with food they had been promised. Prominent trader Andrew J. Myrick declared, "So far as I am concerned, if they [Indians] are hungry, let them eat grass." The Sioux attacked Minnesota settlements and the uprising quickly spread to the eastern Dakotas. The uprising was defeated and 303 Sioux were sentenced to be hanged. President Abraham Lincoln overturned most of the execution orders, but 38 Indians were hanged, the largest mass execution in American history. Little Crow and his followers escaped to Canada.

1863 ◆ Nez Percé and the "Thief Treaty"
The Nez Percé of Oregon and Idaho attempted to live in peace with settlers. In 1860, however, gold was discovered on their land. The U.S. government forced a treaty on the Nez Percé that reduced their land to one-tenth its former size. A small group of Nez Percé accepted the "Thief Treaty," but the majority of the tribe, led by Chief Joseph, refused. "If we ever owned the land we own it still for we never sold it," Chief Joseph said. *(Also see entry dated 1877: Nez Percé War.)*

1863-72 ◆ Cochise and Apache Wars
Cochise, an Apache warrior, led his people in a series of conflicts known as the Apache Wars. From his stronghold in the Dragoon Mountains (located in southern Arizona), Cochise led an effective campaign against U.S. and Mexican forces. In 1871 Cochise opposed efforts to relocate his people to a reservation in New Mexico. In 1872 he finally agreed not to attack the U.S. Army in exchange for reservation land in eastern Arizona.

1864 ◆ Long Walk of the Navajo
The Navajo, angry over losing part of their territory through a treaty signed in 1858, attacked Fort Defiance, located in the middle of their territory. They were defeated and forced to march 800 miles to a 40-square-mile reserve at Fort Sumner, New Mexico. Two thousand died along the way from starvation and exposure (lack of shelter). The 9,000 survivors found themselves on land that lacked

Artist Robert Lindneux's portrait of the Sand Creek Massacre. The painting shows the American flag Chief Black Kettle raised above his tepee in a vain attempt to signal his peaceful intentions.

water and had poor soil. The nearest available wood was five to 18 miles away. Hordes of grasshoppers swept the area. The Navajo called the reservation *Hweedli* (prison).

On this land, the Navajo were expected to become farmers! The U.S. government did little to help the Navajo until a Santa Fe newspaper wrote about the terrible conditions on the reservation. As a result the government allowed the Navajo to return to a small portion (10 percent) of their original homeland. In later years more land was added as the Navajo population grew.

November 29, 1864 ◆ Sand Creek Massacre

Colonel John Chivington led a force from Colorado in an unprovoked attack on a Southern Cheyenne and Arapaho camp, killing an estimated 500 men, women, and children. The Sand Creek Massacre, as it became known, was one of the bloodiest and cruelest events of the Civil War and led to public outcries against such needless brutalities. Although punishment of the parties responsible for the massacre was demanded by the public and by a U.S. congressional committee, no such action was taken.

1866 ◆ Chief Seattle died

Oratory, or speechmaking, was one of the most widely known forms of Native oral literature. Native American cultures have always placed a high value upon public-speaking abilities. One of the most noted of orators was Chief Sealth (also known as Chief Seattle, after whom the city in Washington state is named), a Duwamish-Suquamish tribal leader who died in 1866. One of Chief Sealth's speeches is widely quoted for its environmental message that all people, plants, and animals on earth are related. Sealth, who signed a treaty agreeing to the relocation of his people to a reservation without a fight, was also known for his steadfast adherence to the peaceful settlement of conflicts.

1866 ◆ Montana Gold Rush

Non-Indians began to flood into Montana after gold was discovered. Many miners took the Bozeman Trail from Fort Laramie, Wyoming, to Virginia City, Montana. This trail ran through the lands of the Oglala and Brule Sioux, who fought to keep miners out of the region. The U.S. Army established forts along the Bozeman Trail to protect the miners. *(Also see entry dated April 29, 1868: Treaty of Fort Laramie.)*

1867 ◆ United States bought Alaska

The U.S. government purchased Alaska from Russia. The purchase did not change the situation of the Aleuts, Inuit, and Indians living in Alaska except that they were now under the control of the U.S. government.

July 1, 1867 ◆ Canada formed early government

Canada began to form its own government when New Brunswick and Nova Scotia joined with Quebec as a confederation; other provinces joined the confederation through the rest of the century.

Unlike U.S. Indian groups, most Canadian aboriginal (native) groups did not engage in drawn-out battles with the Canadian government. In fact, after the American Revolution, many dissatisfied U.S. Native groups moved to Canada to escape the oppression they faced at home. By the mid- to late 1800s, however, the Canadian government, like the U.S. government, had placed many restrictions upon Canada's First Nations, denying them rights to self-government and rejecting their land claims. Assimilation policies (policies that tried to force aboriginal peoples to become more like mainstream society in Canada) were also imposed.

July 20, 1867 ◆ Peace Commission Act

The Peace Commission Act was passed by the U.S. Congress, calling for the president to appoint a commission to meet with hostile Indian tribes. Placing Indians on reservations became national policy in the United States after the Civil War, despite the fact that reservations had met with only limited success. The Peace Commission met with many tribes, concluding treaties and establishing reservations. Some tribes agreed to stay on reservation, while others did not.

In 1970, eighty-five years after Louis Riel, Jr., was hanged for treason, Canada issued this stamp honoring him.

1868 • *Poems*

The first volume of poetry published by an American Indian was released. *Poems* was written by the Cherokee writer John Rollin Ridge.

April 29, 1868 • Treaty of Fort Laramie

When gold was discovered in Montana, U.S. settlers began moving through Indian land on what was known as the Bozeman Trail. The Sioux began to attack forts set up along the trail and effectively stopped this travel. The Sioux finally agreed to the Treaty of Fort Laramie which preserved for the Indians the western half of South Dakota, a small section of North Dakota, and the entire Powder River country (present-day Montana). The treaty also called for the U.S. Army to abandon it forts along the Bozeman Trail. This treaty marked one of the few times when the Indians were victorious in war and able to force the U.S. government to accept their peace terms. *(Also see entry dated 1866: Montana Gold Rush.)*

1869 • Gradual Enfranchisement Act

The Canadian government laid out the procedure by which Indians could become citizens. Government officials also began to remove traditional leaders who opposed government policies and replace them with elected band councils. The act also stated that Indian women and their children would lose their Indian status when they married non-Indians, a policy that would not be changed until the 1980s. *(Also see entry dated 1857: Gradual Civilization Act in Canada.)*

1869 • The Red River Métis form provisional government

By the mid-1800s many Métis groups had migrated onto Canada's Plains, where they hunted and traded with the fur trading companies. At this time the Métis considered themselves a distinct nation of peoples, descended mostly from French-Cree or French-Ojibway ancestors. They were French-speaking and Roman Catholic.

In 1869 the Hudson's Bay Company was in the process of selling Métis lands on the Plains to the Canadian government, and Europeans began to settle there. The Métis did not believe that Canada had the right to annex the region without the residents' consent. Fearing that their religion, language, and land would be threatened by large groups of English-speaking Protestants from Ontario who settled in their area, the Red River Métis responded as a nation to intrusions. In October 1869, 16 Métis led by Louis Riel, Jr., stopped Canadian surveyors who were working on transferring lands from the Hudson's Bay Company to the government. A month later, Riel and his forces took possession of Upper Fort Garry, the control center of the Red River Colony. In December 1869 Riel led the Métis in establishing a provisional (temporary) government in order to negotiate the terms under which they, as a nation, would enter Canada.

1869-71 ◆ First Native American appointed as commissioner of Indian affairs

Brigadier General Ely Parker, a Seneca tribal leader and close friend of President Ulysses S. Grant, was appointed commissioner of Indian affairs. It was the first time an Indian had held this post. As commissioner, Parker worked to rid the bureau of corruption. He also began a policy of providing Indians with food and clothing in exchange for their acceptance of living on reservations.

1870 ◆ First Ghost Dance Movement

Wodziwob, a Paiute Indian living on the California/Nevada border, was credited with beginning the Ghost Dance religion. Wodziwob was informed by the Creator that non-Ghost Dancers would be swallowed up by a great earthquake. Indians would be spared or resurrected in three days so that they could live as they had before European contact. This vision was especially appealing to Indians at that time, offering a sense of comfort and a focus on the old ways of life. With all the death, disease, and violence Native peoples had experienced since the arrival of Europeans on the American continents, it probably did seem like the world was ending.

LOUIS RIEL, JR., AND THE MÉTIS

Louis Riel, Jr., was born on October 22, 1844 to a French-Ojibway (Métis) man and a French Canadian woman at the Métis community at the Red River colony in present-day Manitoba, Canada. After his education at the colony and then the Collége de Montreal, he traveled extensively through the United States. In 1868 Riel returned to the Red River colony. The following year he led the Red River Métis in their resistance to the Canadian government. In August 1870 he fled to the United States, fearing arrest. He was elected to the federal House of Commons in 1873 and 1874 but never took his seat there.

In the late 1870s, Riel had a nervous breakdown and spent some time in a mental institution, from which he was released in 1878. He then became a teacher at a mission school in Montana. In 1884 Métis colonies in the Northwest Territories asked Riel to represent them in their grievances against the Canadian government. He set up a provisional (temporary) government in Batoche in 1885. The Canadian government responded severely, quickly crushing the Northwest Rebellion, and Riel was arrested and convicted of treason. On November 16, 1885, he was executed. Riel's execution has remained an emotional and controversial issue in Canada. There have been many calls for his posthumous (after death) pardon, and several statues have been erected in his memory.

Ely Parker, first Indian commissioner of Indian affairs.

The Ghost Dance movement developed a new class of spiritual leaders called dreamer doctors. The movement lasted about two years in California, but it continued to exist in other areas for more than 20 years. *(Also see entry dated 1890: Ghost Dance and Wounded Knee.)*

1870 ♦ *McKay* v. *Campbell*

The U.S. Supreme Court, in the case of *McKay* v. *Campbell,* decided that Indians were not U.S. citizens since their allegiance was to their tribe, not to the United States. Because of this ruling Indians were denied protections guaranteed by the U.S. Constitution.

1870 ♦ Métis's Red River resistance crushed

The Métis provisional government arrested several people for resisting Métis law and in March 1870, one of these prisoners was executed. The Canadian government had been negotiating with the provisional government, and in June, the Manitoba Act was passed. Under the terms of the act, the Canadian government would administer the Northwest Territories—lands acquired from the Hudson's Bay Company and populated by a vast majority of Native peoples. The Métis were guaranteed the right to use the French language, Catholic schools, additional lands, and recognition of their land rights in the province. However, by August, the reaction to the Métis government's execution of the prisoner prompted 1,200 Canadian and British troops to enter Métis lands on a campaign of intimidation. About two-thirds of the Métis population left the Red River area to join other Métis groups. Louis Riel fled to the United States. *(Also see entry dated 1869: The Red River Métis form provisional government.)*

1870-90 ♦ Peyote religion

For centuries Indians in northern Mexico had used the peyote plant in religious ceremonies. Peyote brought on a dreamlike feeling, which followers of the Peyote religion felt moved them closer to the spirit world. In the late nineteenth century the Peyote religion spread among the Arapaho, Cheyenne, Comanche, and Kiowa.

Tribal members developed their own ceremonies, songs, and symbolism. Dreams, prayers, and visions also became part of the Peyote religion. Peyote was taken as a sacrament and followers vowed to follow the Peyote Road. They promised to be trustworthy, honorable, and community-oriented. Family, children, and cultural survival became major parts of this religion. *(Also see entries*

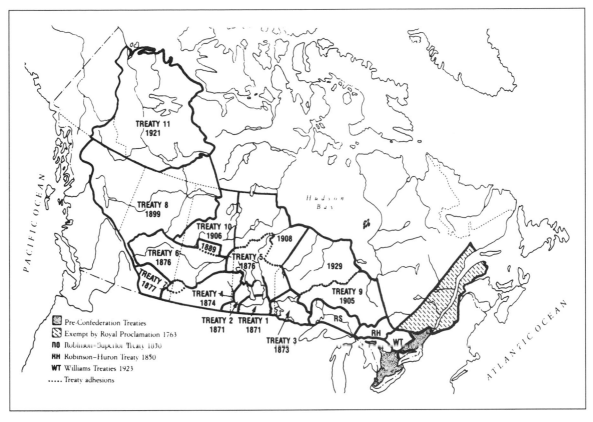

Indian treaty areas
in Canada.

*dated 1918: Native American church established; and April 17, 1990: Oregon
v. Smith.)*

1871 ♦ Canadian "numbered treaties"

Canada wanted to open lands in the West for settlement and eliminate aboriginal (native) claims to those lands. Between 1871 and 1923 the Canadian government signed 11 treaties that covered what are now the provinces of Manitoba, Saskatchewan, Alberta, and northern Ontario and the Mackenzie Valley region of the Northwest Territories. These 11 treaties are often referred to as "numbered treaties" because they are titled "Treaty Number 1," "Treaty Number 2," and so on.

In addition to exchanging land for Indian reserves, the numbered treaties typically guaranteed Indian hunting and fishing rights on land that was given up but remained unoccupied. Provisions were made for education and agricultural development on the reserves, including a system of annuities (annual payments to the bands).

However, there was much debate over what these provisions actually meant to the Indians and to the government. For example, some Indian groups claimed that a university education was a treaty right. Some felt that the Canadian government should provide complete health care because of the "medicine chest" provision in many treaties. "Medicine chest" clauses stated that the government would provide medical supplies to the reserves.

Some Indian leaders argued that, in general, Native people were misled and cheated during the treaty-making process. Therefore, more lands, rights, and benefits were due to them. These leaders believed that the treaties should be renegotiated.

1871 ♦ U.S. treaty era ended

The U.S. Congress ended treaty-making. Congress passed legislation (new laws) to manage Indian affairs. Even though the method of dealing with Indians changed, their legal status (or rights under law) remained the same. After 1871 U.S. presidents made "agreements" with the Indians for the sale of their land, even though treaties were no longer being written. These agreements were basically the same as treaties, but they did not recognize tribes as independent nations.

Regardless of whether the documents they signed were called treaties or agreements, Native nations lost their lands. In fact, at the end of the treaty era, American Indian tribes still controlled one-tenth of the 48 states, or about one-fourth of the land between the Mississippi and the Rocky Mountains. By the early 1900s, much of this land would be owned by the U.S. government. *(Also see entry dated 1853-56: Indian treaties.)*

1874 ♦ Gold discovered in Black Hills

In the summer of 1874 an expedition under Lieutenant Colonel George Armstrong Custer discovered gold in the Black Hills of South Dakota, sacred land for the Lakota Sioux, Cheyenne, and other tribes. In violation of the Fort Laramie Treaty, gold miners flooded the Black Hills. Soon Indian and U.S. Army forces were fighting once again over this land.

1876 ♦ Battle of the Little Bighorn

After gold miners started working in the Black Hills, several bands of Sioux left their reservations to protect the Black Hills from being desecrated (treated in a way that violated the sanctity of these sacred lands). Led by Crazy Horse of the Oglala Sioux and Sitting Bull of the Hunkpapa band of Teton Sioux, the Indians gathered to face the U.S. Army, which was protecting the miners.

The U.S. Army decided to attack the combined Indian forces. The Seventh Cavalry, commanded by Lieutenant Colonel George Armstrong Custer, was sent to the southern end of Little Bighorn Valley, in present-day eastern Montana. It

The view of the Little Bighorn Valley from the position of the Seventh Cavalry looking in the direction of the Sioux, Cheyenne, and Arapaho encampments.

was here that Custer discovered a large group of Indians. He decided to attack but split his forces, leaving him with 225 men. Sioux and Cheyenne warriors met Custer's attack; in the battle that followed they killed every U.S. soldier, including Custer. The Battle of the Little Bighorn, or Custer's Last Stand, was one of the worst defeats suffered by U.S. Army forces in their battles against Indian nations.

The army pursued the Sioux after the Battle of the Little Bighorn. In 1877 they arrested and then killed Crazy Horse. Sitting Bull and parts of the Sioux tribe fled to Canada and did not return to the Dakotas until 1881. *(Also see entries dated 1874: Gold discovered in Black Hills; June 2, 1877: Sitting Bull in Canada; and September 5, 1877: Crazy Horse killed.)*

1876 ◆ Indian Act in Canada

The Indian Act was designed to administer Indian affairs and to promote the assimilation (blending into mainstream culture) of Canada's First Nations. It established a reserve system (similar to United States reservations), in which reserves were often governed by voluntary elected band councils with the kind of powers usually granted to Canada's city governments. These councils, forced on many tribes by the Canadian government, were seen by many as part of an effort to destroy traditional Indian governments. The Indian Act did not, and still does not, recognize Canadian Indians as retaining any right to self-government.

With the passage of the Indian Act, Native peoples in Canada were divided into three groups: status, treaty, and non-status Indians. These categories affected the benefits or rights Indians were given by the government.

A status Indian was a person who was registered with the government as an Indian. Status Indians were members of the 633 recognized bands across Canada. A treaty Indian was a person who was a registered member of a band that signed a treaty or a person who could prove he or she was descended from such a band.

Non-status Indians were people who were Indian but who had lost their right to be registered under the Indian Act as status Indians. In the past, the most common reason for losing the right to be a status Indian had been marriage of a registered Indian to a non-Indian.

1877 ◆ Nez Percé War

After the defeat of Custer at Little Bighorn, the army ordered that all nonreservation Nez Percé be placed on reservations. The Nez Percé agreed to travel to reservations, but along the way to their new home in Montana, a skirmish between some young Nez Percé warriors and the army developed into the Nez Percé War. After a defeat in Montana, the Nez Percé moved on to Wyoming, where they hoped to join the Crow. The Crow rejected them and so the Nez Percé tried to reach the Canadian border. They were attacked again by the U.S. Army only 40 miles from the border and forced to surrender. The Nez Percé were promised that they would not be punished for resisting the army and would be allowed to live on a reservation in Idaho. The U.S. government, however, sent them to Kansas as prisoners of war.

Throughout this struggle Nez Percé Chief Joseph urged the U.S. government to live up to their original agreement. In 1879 he traveled to Washington, D.C., to make his case. In 1885 the U.S. government finally allowed the Nez Percé to move to a reservation in Idaho, but Chief Joseph was forced to move to the Colville Reservation in north-central Washington. For years he tried to purchase land in his homeland, the *Wallowa,* the Place of Winding Waters, but settlers living there refused to sell him any land. He died in 1904. *(Also see entry dated 1863: Nez Percé and the "Thief Treaty.")*

June 2, 1877 ◆ Sitting Bull in Canada

Sitting Bull and about a thousand of his followers arrived in Canada after defeating U.S. forces at the battle of the Little Bighorn River on June 25, 1876. They remained in Canada until 1881, when, facing starvation, they returned to the United States. *(Also see entry dated 1876: Battle of the Little Bighorn.)*

September 5, 1877 ◆ Crazy Horse killed

Crazy Horse, a Sioux warrior, was captured in 1877. Crazy Horse became famous at the Battle of the Little Bighorn and led his people in several other brilliant campaigns against U.S. troops. On May 6, 1877, Crazy Horse reluctantly surrendered because his people were starving and weary of battle. Crazy Horse was killed during an attempt to confine him to a guardhouse. *(Also see entry dated 1876: Battle of the Little Bighorn.)*

1877-83 ◆ Northern Cheyenne escaped

In 1877 the Northern Cheyenne tribe, then living in present-day Montana and the western Dakotas, surrendered to U.S. troops and reluctantly agreed to move to Indian Territory (present-day Oklahoma). Later that same year Chief Dull Knife led his people out of Indian Territory, planning to return to their homeland. This escape convinced the U.S. government that it was impossible to make Indians stay in Indian Territory if they wanted to leave. U.S. Indian policymakers abandoned the attempt to relocate Indian nations to Indian Territory and allowed them to take reservations within their home territories. In 1003 the Northern Cheyenne were granted a reservation in eastern Montana.

1879 ◆ Carlisle Indian School founded

The Carlisle Indian School was founded in Pennsylvania in an effort to show that Indians could be educated in the ways of American culture. Other schools were founded in Arizona, California, New Mexico, Oklahoma, and Oregon and on various Indian reservations.

Sitting Bull, Hunkpapa Sioux tribal leader.

U.S. reformers took Indian children from their homes and communities in the belief that it would be in the interest of the children to destroy their Native culture, languages, and traditions. When the children reached first grade, government agents took them from their families and sent them to Indian boarding schools. Schools were run by the Bureau of Indian Affairs and allowed little or no local control. Government teachers forced Indian children to learn English and punished them with whippings and denying them food when they broke the rules and used their Native language. Indian education was limited to vocational studies—since Indians were not considered to be intelligent enough to learn professional skills—but children were taught some academic skills. Boys were taught blacksmithing and tailoring, while girls learned sewing, ironing, and laundering.

Before European colonists arrived on the continent, most Native North American children learned by watching and doing. The entire community served as their teachers: parents, older brothers and sisters, relatives, and elders. Through the community the children learned language, customs, traditions, and values—things that were useful and meaningful to them in their way of life. When the children became adults, they were expected to teach the next generation, just as they had been taught.

1879-82 ◆ Reform groups founded

The Women's National Indian Association, founded in 1879, and the Indian Rights Association, founded in Philadelphia by Quakers and other Christian reformers in 1882, were non-Indian groups formed to help Native Americans in the United States.

These groups, and a number of others that followed, wanted to preserve Indian cultures and improve living conditions. Although they helped Native Americans, their goals in certain areas differed from the wishes of some of the tribes with whom they worked. One of the goals of these early organizations was to help Indians blend into mainstream American society. Many Indians, however, sought to preserve their own way of life and did not wish to adopt U.S. culture.

1880s ◆ Extermination of the buffalo on the Plains

The importance of the buffalo to Plains people and their cultures could not be overstated. Every part of the animal was put to use, and food, shelter, and clothing were all provided by the buffalo. American leaders began to see that they could destroy the Indians by destroying the buffalo. U.S. Congressman James Garrison claimed that the secretary of the interior once told him that he would "rejoice as far as the Indian matter was concerned when the last buffalo was killed."

The slaughter did not take long to complete. By the late nineteenth century non-Indian hunters had destroyed the large herds of buffalo; in fact, there were only about 1,000 buffalo left at that time. Buffalo were killed for their tongue meat and their hides. Without adequate supplies of buffalo for food, the Indian Plains Culture could not survive. Often faced with the threat of starvation, Plains Indians had little choice but to move to the reservations, where they were dependent on the United States for food and supplies.

90

1880s ✦ Susette La Flesche

Susette La Flesche (Bright Eyes in her native language) of the Omaha tribe devoted much of her life to working for women's and Indian rights. In 1879 and 1880 La Flesche made a speaking tour of the eastern United States. In 1881 she married philanthropist and journalist Thomas H. Tibbles. Throughout the late 1880s, La Flesche and her husband made numerous public appearances, including trips to England and Scotland, where they pleaded for improvement in the condition of the Omaha and Ponca tribes. La Flesche and her husband edited The *Weekly Independent,* a populist newspaper in Lincoln, Nebraska. La Flesche also coauthored *Ploughed Under: The Story of an Indian Chief.*

Group of Omaha boys in cadet uniforms, Carlisle Indian School, 1880.

1881-84 ✦ *A Century of Dishonor* published

Renowned historical novelist Helen Hunt Jackson, in *A Century of Dishonor,* wrote a severe attack on U.S. Indian policy and the treatment of American Indians in U.S. society. Because of her work, the U.S. Congress formed a special commission to investigate and suggest reforms of Indian affairs. Jackson's research on the special commission provided her with material to write a biographical novel, *Ramona,* about the life of a California Indian woman. This book created considerable interest in the United States about the plight of Indians.

1882 ✦ Hopi reservation formed

Because the Hopi never entered into open fighting with the United States, no treaty was ever signed to give them legal title to their homelands. The Navajo, whose lands encircled the Hopi lands, entered into a treaty with the United States for their lands in northwestern New Mexico and northeastern Arizona. In 1882 the Hopi complained that Navajo families were settling on their lands. The Hopi reservation was then established by executive order (an order by the president), but Hopi lands continued to be settled by Navajo and Mormons.

1883-84 ✦ Sarah Winnemucca toured the East

Sarah Winnemucca of the Paiute tribe was active as a peacemaker, teacher, and defender of her people. From 1883 to 1884 Winnemucca made a speaking tour of the East, often dressed as an Indian princess to draw crowds.

While in the East, Winnemucca met with many important sympathizers of Indian rights and published *Life among the Paiutes, Their Wrongs and Claims*.

In her book Winnemucca spoke out strongly against the way the Paiutes were treated by the Indian agents and non-Native settlers and described the virtues of her people's traditional ways and the need for government reform to protect the Paiutes and other tribes. Winnemucca returned to Nevada and founded a school for Indians. She died of tuberculosis at the age of 47.

April 19, 1884 ◆ Potlatches banned
The Canadian government banned potlatches, elaborate gift-giving ceremonies held among many Native groups of the Pacific Coast. The government was worried that the potlatches were helping Indians oppose the Canadian government.

1885 ◆ Second Métis provisional government
Louis Riel returned to the Northwest Territories in Canada and formed the second Métis provisional government at Batoche. Canadian troops moved toward Batoche, but the Métis were able to resist them for over a month. On May 12, 1885, after a three-day battle, the Métis were defeated, and were once more forced to flee the area. Riel surrendered and was hanged for treason for his role in the rebellion. The Métis considered him a martyr for their cause. French Canadians also protested the execution. The hanging of Riel served to sustain Métis nationalism for the next century and the question of Riel's innocence or guilt became the center of one of the most controversial and divisive debates in Canadian history.

1885-86 ◆ Sitting Bull joined Wild West Show
Sitting Bull joined William (Buffalo Bill) Cody's Wild West Show, a traveling exhibition of "Indian fighters" and "Indian War Chiefs." In 1886 Sitting Bull left the show and returned to Standing Rock Reservation. In his remaining years, he continued to oppose the breakup of Sioux land and the assimilation (the blending in) of Indians into U.S. culture.

Late 1800s ◆ Reservations in the Northwest
Through the late 1800s, non-Native settlement of the Northwest Coast progressed at a staggering rate. During this settlement period, treaties were signed with the United States, reservation communities were established in British Columbia, and the number of Native villages in Alaska shrank to a few. At this time the Native population rapidly declined because of European diseases to which the Native peoples had no immunity. By 1900 non-Natives outnumbered Natives in most areas, and the Native societies were overtaken by the growing dominant culture.

As non-Natives controlled more of the area, Northwest Coast peoples found it difficult to continue to fish, hunt, and gather as they had in the past. Fishing,

A late nineteenth-century photograph showing totem poles built in front of the large houses of the Haida village of Skidgate, on Queen Charlotte Islands, British Columbia.

logging, and farming became the area's main economic activities. Conflicts over uses of the land arose between Natives and non Natives. As traditional activities and resources became limited, Native people sought wage labor in nearby non-Native communities.

1886 ◆ Geronimo surrendered

One of the most feared and respected of Apache leaders, Geronimo became a warrior after his wife and children were killed by Mexican soldiers. From that point onward, his life was filled with a succession of military raids, captures, escapes, and brief attempts to live on Indian reservations. Although constantly pursued, Geronimo eluded the larger U.S. forces until 1886, when he was forced to surrender. Newspapers, presidents, and politicians called for Geronimo's execution but instead he was imprisoned. In 1894 Geronimo and many of his close Apache friends were moved to Fort Sill, Oklahoma, where he died in 1909, still a prisoner of war.

1887 ✦ Dawes Act

The U.S. Congress passed the General Allotment Act, also known as the Dawes Act. This act called for the allotment of tribal lands (meaning that land would be parceled out to individuals, not controlled by the tribe). Under allotment, tribes would no longer own their lands in common (as a group) in the traditional way. Instead, land would be assigned to individuals. The head of a family would receive 160 acres, and other family members would get smaller pieces of land.

From the point of view of most Native American cultures, allotment took away Native peoples' control of their lives and lands. Many Indians could not make a living off the parcels of land they had been given. They had not chosen the way of life that they were forced into. Many Indians sold their lands as soon as possible, in order to get money for survival. In many cases, whites bought Indian lands illegally and the government did little or nothing to stop them.

Allotment, along with conversion to Christianity and farming, was supposed to bring Indians into the mainstream of American life. Once on the reservations, many Indian peoples attempted to become farmers. But most were unable to harvest enough to live on, because much of the land was not fertile. Indians lacked the money to purchase farm equipment and were unable to borrow money from the bank. Large-scale commercial farming was therefore impossible.

As an alternative, the U.S. government encouraged cattle ranching. Some groups were successful cattle ranchers. The Blackfeet, for example, registered over 400 brands of cattle by the year 1900. Cattle buyers in Chicago purchased animals from both the Blackfeet and Northern Cheyenne reservations.

1889 ✦ Oklahoma land runs

The famous Oklahoma land runs opened Indian Territory to non-Natives. These were spectacular one-day chances to acquire former Indian lands. At noon on April 22, an estimated 50,000 people lined up at the boundaries of the Indian Territory. They claimed two million acres of land. By nightfall, there were tent cities, banks, and stores doing business there.

Most Oklahoma Indian tribes were resettled in Oklahoma against their wishes in the 1800s under the U.S. removal policies. Most of the land that is now Oklahoma was then called "Indian Territory" and was to be set aside solely for Indian use. During the 1830s, when much of the relocating of Native groups to Indian Territory was taking place, a proposal was under way which would have made Indian Territory a commonwealth to be governed by a confederation of the tribes living there. But the government failed to protect Native American rights even in Indian Territory. The Oklahoma land run caused the loss of most Oklahoma Indian lands that were fertile or rich in minerals.

In 1890 the Oklahoma Organic Act reduced Indian Territory to the eastern portion of the territory. The act created Oklahoma Territory in the western portion, and there established a non-Indian U.S. territorial government. *(Also see entry dated November 16, 1907: Five Civilized Tribes school systems closed.)*

1890s ✦ Alaska Gold Rush

Native North Americans in Alaska were very isolated, even after the United States purchased the territory from Russia in 1867. The Alaska Gold Rush in the 1890s changed this situation rapidly. Settlers flooded in, and Native people began to find work in fishing, logging, and other jobs. Many adopted Christianity. Formal education became widespread.

U.S. expansion into Alaska was also motivated by fur. Although Congress had passed laws to protect Native lands, there was little to prevent non-Natives from building there. Fish canneries, gold mining camps, trade and manufacturing sites, railroads, timber harvesting, homesteads, towns—all came to Alaska in the late 1800s and early 1900s.

1890 ✦ Ghost Dance and Wounded Knee

Many Indian nations in the West were concerned that their way of life was being threatened. Death

Wovoka, the prophet of the second Ghost Dance.

from diseases brought by settlers was widespread. On the Plains the buffalo and other game were declining. In response to these concerns, the second Ghost Dance movement arose.

The Ghost Dance movement was initiated by Wovoka, the son of a Paiute shaman, or religious leader. Wovoka had a vision from the Great Spirit in which the Ghost Dance was revealed to him. "When the sun died," Wovoka said, "I went up to heaven and saw God and all the people who had died a long time ago. God told me to come back and tell my people they must be good and love one another, and not fight, or steal, or lie. He gave me this dance to give to my people."

The Ghost Dance included many Paiute traditions, such as the Round Dance. This dance was performed to achieve successful transition to the next world after death. In some versions, the dance was to help bring back to earth many dead ancestors and to replenish game. It was hoped that these rituals would restore Indians to their former, more prosperous condition before the invasion of non-Native settlers.

Wovoka encouraged the Great Basin peoples to follow the teachings he had received in a vision from the Great Spirit. He urged them to love one another

Burial of the Dead
at the Battle of Wounded Knee S.D.
Copy Righted Jan 1st 1891 by the
North Western Photo Co
Chadron Neb
No 1

After the massacre at Wounded Knee, 146 bodies were buried in a mass grave on a small hill.

and live in peace with everyone. His teachings were probably a mixture of his traditional beliefs and Christian thought, with which he was familiar.

The Ghost Dance religion spread to many tribes throughout the West. In 1889 many Sioux were dying of starvation as a result of a drought (lack of rain). Although the U.S. Congress promised food rations, they were delayed in arriving while people went hungry. Epidemics ravaged the reservations. Some Sioux turned Wovoka's teachings into a movement calling for violence. Soldiers, settlers, government agents, and missionaries feared for their lives as rumors spread that the Ghost Dance was encouraging the Sioux to fight again, like at Little

Bighorn, for their rights and freedom. The Office of Indian Affairs outlawed the Ghost Dance, and the U.S. government strengthened the army on the northern Plains.

When Sitting Bull was suspected of supporting the Ghost Dance, reservation policemen arrested him. As he was being captured, a fight broke out and Sitting Bull was killed. In reaction to his death, a group of Sioux Ghost Dancers, led by Big Foot, retreated to a site on the Pine Ridge Reservation known as Wounded Knee. They were pursued by army troops. After some misunderstandings about what the Ghost Dancers intended to do, the army fired on the Sioux with machine guns and killed Indian men, women, and children. Three hundred seventy Indians were killed, 250 of them women and children. This incident was known as the Wounded Knee Massacre. After the massacre, the Ghost Dance movement declined. *(Also see entry dated 1870: First Ghost Dance Movement.)*

1890-1900 ◆ "Vanishing Americans"
At the end of the nineteenth century, most non-Indians believed that Native Americans as a group would not long survive, and therefore the term "Vanishing Americans" came to be applied to them. Often this idea was used to justify taking away Native lands and moving the people to places far away. From an estimated population of 15 million in 1500, the American Indian population had declined to a low point of 237,196 in the 1900 U.S. Census. After 1900, however, the population slowly recovered.

1890-1934 ◆ Assimilationist Policy
The U.S. government declared its policy of assimilating Indians into mainstream society. In other words, government officials wanted Native peoples to give up their own ways of life and to blend in with the rest of American society. Part of the reason for this policy may have been a genuine belief that assimilated Native Americans would find equal treatment and receive a fairer share of the nation's wealth if they were not isolated from the mainstream. But the policy of assimilation was also supported by racism (the belief that, because of racial differences, a group of people is inferior to one's own group). Because many Americans had little understanding of American Indian cultural traditions, they simply perceived them as inferior to white ways. Racist attitudes were used to justify forcing the Indians to give up their life-styles, beliefs, and land.

Many Americans, who were busy building a commercial society centered around industry and agricultural production, felt that Indians "wasted" land by hunting and trading over large areas. The government hoped that if Indians could be trained to farm small areas, they would no longer need so much land. If they needed less land for survival, then they would be more willing to sell it to the United States.

After 1890 most Indian nations were located on reservations or were not recognized by the federal government. The policy of allotment led to the loss of Indian land, and since most reservation economies could not support the Indian peoples, reservation residents became economically and politically dependent on the Bureau of Indian Affairs (BIA) and its agents. Food, clothing, medicine, education, and ceremonial life were strictly controlled. Traditional governments were not allowed to operate, and ceremonies, like the Sun Dance, were prohibited.

By the 1890s the BIA had undermined the ability of Indians to support and govern themselves. The BIA assigned agents to run the reservations. These Indian agents often controlled the people with the help of the more "Americanized" tribal leaders. Power was transferred to these leaders, who were often manipulated by the BIA to serve U.S. policy rather than the interests of the tribe. In some cases, the Indian leaders were corrupt and used their position to serve their own needs, rather than those of the community. As a result, Native Americans were frequently unable to trust the leadership of their reservations.

Children were sent to boarding schools, where they could not speak their native language. Federal policymakers hoped to reeducate Indian children and make them part of U.S. society and then abolish the reservations. Many Plains Indians resisted by keeping their children home. More rules regarding attendance were put in place and the government denied food to families who did not send their children to school. By this time Indian people on reservations depended almost totally on the government for food rations, so cutting off their supply was a powerful tool.

The policy of assimilation was not successful. Many Indian students at the federal boarding schools felt lonely and longed to return home, while others adjusted to the new life and returned to the reservations only after they had finished school. Very few returned to the reservations in order to influence others to adopt an "American" lifestyle.

The policy of moving children off the reservations was changed and more boarding schools were established on reservations. These were less expensive to operate. Also, although most Indian parents did not object to the education itself, they did not want to lose contact with their children. It was hoped that if the schools were located closer to the families, parents would be more willing to send their children. By 1892 the U.S. government was operating more than 100 Indian boarding schools, both on and off reservations.

1894 ♦ *The Sioux Ghost Dance*

The film *The Sioux Ghost Dance,* made by the (Thomas) Edison Studios, was the first known motion picture recording of American Indians. This short silent film showed five Sioux Indians dressed in breechcloths and head feathers, beating on drums and dancing on a stage.

A fourth grade class in an Indian boarding school in Genoa, Nebraska, 1910.

In film American Indians were usually portrayed in one of two ways — as either "noble savages" (proud, independent, and honorable) or "bloodthirsty savages" (attacking and scalping innocent white settlers). These images represented the viewpoint of the non-Natives who wrote and produced the films.

Occasionally, films showed cultural aspects of Native life, and some dealt with issues such as Indian and non-Indian marriages, racism, or separation from one's culture.

1897–1930 ◆ Edward Curtis photographed the "Vanishing Race"

Believing he was witnessing the passing of the traditional Indian way of life, American photographer Edward Curtis became determined to preserve the Native culture through photography and his detailed notes about diverse Indian cultures. For 30 years, beginning around the turn of the century, Curtis attempted to photograph the Indian tribes west of the Mississippi from New Mexico to Alaska, studying more than 80 tribes, recording over 10,000 songs, and taking 40,000 photographs. His photographs were published in 20 volumes of *North American Indian* and *Indian Days of the Long Ago*.

Early 1900s ◆ Struggle and change in the twentieth century

The early years of the twentieth century were difficult times for Native Americans. Many groups continued to feel the disastrous effects of the Dawes Act of 1887, which cut up their lands, often into small, unworkable allotments. Federal, state, and county officials often worked with the railroads, cattle ranchers, miners, and oil and timber companies to take away Indian lands and resources.

Hunting, fishing, gathering food, and farming continued on the reservations, but it was impossible for most Native groups to support themselves through these efforts. For this reason many Native Americans became wage earners. Indians worked as migrant workers (moving from place to place with the changing crops) in labor camps and on ranches, performing a variety of low-paying jobs. Sometimes the Bureau of Indian Affairs hired a reservation's police officers and judges from among its people. And some Indians received an income from renting their land to non-Indian farmers and ranchers.

1902 ◆ Charles Eastman

Charles Eastman, a Santee Sioux, wrote two autobiographies, *Indian Boyhood* (1902) and *From Deep Woods to Civilization* (1916). He also wrote many books on Dakota culture. Eastman's autobiographies described his life before contact with non-Indians at age 15, as well as his education and career. He was a YMCA and Boy Scout leader and organizer, a public lecturer and writer, and a medical doctor on two reservations. As physician at the Pine Ridge Reservation at the time of the Wounded Knee Massacre in 1890, when the U.S. Cavalry killed nearly 300 Sioux, mostly unarmed women and children, Eastman provided a valuable historical record of that disaster. Throughout his life he worked to further the causes of American Indians. Eastman spent over 20 years trying to restore the treaty rights of his people.

1902 ◆ *Lone Wolf* v. *Hitchcock*.

In this case the U.S. Supreme Court ruled that the U.S. Congress had the power to ignore or change Indian treaties. This decision was a major blow to Indian land rights.

1903 ◆ Charles "Chief" Bender, Chippewa Major League pitcher

Charles "Chief" Bender, a Chippewa, started his Major League baseball career with the Philadelphia Athletics of the American League. A member of the Baseball Hall of Fame, Bender won 208 games and lost 111 in a 16-year career.

Geronimo and three of his warriors photographed in 1886, after their defeat.

1906 ◆ Charles Curtis elected to Senate

Charles Curtis, a Kaw Indian from Kansas, was the first Native American to be elected to the U.S. Senate. He had served in the U.S. House of Representatives from 1892 until 1906 and then served in the Senate from 1907 to 1913 and from 1915 to 1929. *(Also see entry dated 1928: Charles Curtis elected vice president.)*

1906 ◆ *Geronimo's Story of His Life*

Dictated by the famous Apache leader, this autobiography represents one of the most historically important American Indian literary productions. By the time the book was begun Geronimo and his followers had been prisoners of war for over 20 years. The book documented the history of the resistance of the Apache people.

November 16, 1907 ◆ Indian Territory became Oklahoma

The state of Oklahoma was admitted to the United States. The name Oklahoma came from the Choctaw word Okla Homma, translated as "Home of the Red

People." Most Indian governments in the former Indian Territory had been abolished, including the constitutional governments of the Cherokee, Chickasaw, Choctaw, Creek, and Seminole (the Five Civilized Tribes). Indian land was assigned to individuals, not tribes, and many Indians lost their land as a result of debt, legal fraud, or inability to pay taxes. Oklahoma citizens urged that the remaining Indian lands be put on the market and that Indian landholdings be taxed. The promise of a free Indian commonwealth or state had dissolved.

More than 67 tribes existed in Oklahoma. Only a few of these tribes (probably fewer than six) had lived in Oklahoma before European contact. Since Oklahoma became a state, Indian tribes have tried to keep their status as self-governing and independent communities, except for limitations placed on them by treaties, agreements, or laws. *(Also see entry dated 1889: Oklahoma land runs.)*

November 17, 1907 ✦ Five Civilized Tribes school system closed
In the late 1700s the Cherokee, Chickasaw, Choctaw, Creek, and Seminole nations of the Southeast responded to government interference in the education of their children by developing their own schools. The Cherokee people had developed a syllabary that presented the Cherokee language in print. With their writing system, Cherokee people had a higher literacy rate (the percentage of people who could read and write) than the settlers who lived nearby.

The many accomplishments of the Southeastern tribes in such areas as government and education earned them the title "The Five Civilized Tribes." Despite their achievements, the five tribes were forced to leave their homelands in the East and Southeast and move to Indian Territory, present-day Oklahoma. The Cherokee re-established their unique educational system in their new lands. When the state of Oklahoma was created, however, the U.S. Congress abolished the Cherokee school system, and Indian control of education was lost once again. Later in the twentieth century many Indian groups established their own community schools, modeled after the school systems of the Five Civilized Tribes. *(Also see entry dated 1971: Five Civilized Tribes.)*

1908 ✦ Louis Tewanima competed in Olympic Games
Louis Tewanima, a Hopi Indian runner from Arizona, competed in the Olympic Games held in London, England. A triple medal winner in the 1908 and 1912 Olympics, he competed in both the 5,000- and 10,000-meter events, as well as the marathon. He became the first athlete elected to the Arizona Sports Hall of Fame.

1910-1960 ✦ "Southwest style" of painting
The "Southwest style" of painting emerged between 1910 and 1960. Southwest style paintings depicted historic ceremonial dances, hunting scenes, and daily activities in a two-dimensional manner, using pale colors.

1911 ✦ Last Indian revolt

The last recorded uprising of Indians occurred when the Shoshoni revolted in Humboldt County, Nevada, murdering some stockmen. A sheriff's posse hunted down the band, killing everyone except a woman and two small children.

March 1911 ✦ Chippewa protested Indian images in movies

A group of Chippewa arrived in Washington, D.C., to protest the movies' alleged distortions of American Indians. They requested that President William H. Taft impose congressional regulations against the industry's stereotyping of Native Americans.

October 1911 ✦ Society of American Indians

At a national conference of Native American leaders, the name Society of American Indians (SAI) was chosen for the group. SAI worked for better educational programs and improved reservation conditions. Internal disputes caused the group to disband in 1923. *(Also see entry dated May 13, 1916: Indian Day.)*

1912 ✦ Founding of the Alaska Native Brotherhood

The Alaska Native Brotherhood was formed. The Brotherhood promoted civil rights issues such as the right to vote, access to public education for Native children, and civil rights in public places such as the right to attend movie theaters. It defended Native workers in Alaskan fish canneries and the rights of Alaskan fishermen. The Brotherhood also fought court battles to win land rights for Native Americans.

1912 ✦ Jim Thorpe won decathlon

Jim Thorpe, from the Sauk and Fox nation, won the decathlon (a competition made up of ten track and field events) at the 1912 Olympic Games held in Stockholm, Sweden. Thorpe's medal was later taken away from him, however, because he had played semi-professional baseball. (At the time, only amateur— or unpaid—athletes could participate in the Olympics.) After the Olympics Thorpe played professional baseball from 1913 to 1919 with a career batting average of .252. He then went on to play professional football and became the first president of the American Professional Football Association. Thorpe was named to both the college and professional football halls of fame. Jim Thorpe died in 1953. In 1954 a town in Pennsylvania was renamed in his honor. After his death, many Americans from all walks of life began a campaign to have his Olympic medals restored. Thirty-one years after his death, and seventy-two years after the Stockholm event, replicas of his medals were returned to his daughter Charlotte during the 1984 Olympics in Los Angeles.

Young men from File Hills Indian Colony in Saskatchewan, Canada, who enlisted for service during World War I, posing with their fathers before leaving for battle.

1913 ✦ Buffalo head nickel issued

The U.S. government issued the famous "Buffalo head" Indian nickel. The nickel contained a portrait of 13 Indian chiefs, including John Big Tree of the Iroquois, Iron Tall of the Sioux, and Two Moons of the Cheyenne.

1914-18 ✦ World War I

Up to 4,000 Indians, approximately 35 percent of those eligible, volunteered to fight for Canada in World War I. As noncitizens, Indians were not eligible for the draft and did not qualify for all the veterans' benefits that non-Natives did.

The United States entered World War I in 1917. Despite not being subject to the draft law, more than 8,000 Indians volunteered to serve in the war. Indian contributions to the war effort became an important factor in the U.S. Congress's decision to pass the Indian Citizenship Act of 1924. *(Also see entry dated June 2, 1924: Indians granted U.S. citizenship.)*

February 1915 ◆ Allied Tribes of British Columbia
Native Americans in the Canadian province of British Columbia formed the Allied Tribes of British Columbia to protect their land rights. British Columbia Indians were the first in Canada to establish political organizations to represent them. The provincial government of British Columbia refused to negotiate land claims with Native Americans until the 1980s.

May 13, 1916 ◆ Indian Day
Sponsored by the Society of American Indians, May 13 was established as Indian Day. The purpose of this day was to recognize and honor the American Indian and to improve the conditions of Indian people. *(Also see entry dated October 1911: Society of American Indians.)*

c. 1916-1920s ◆ Pueblo artists began watercolor painting
A small group of young Pueblo artists began painting with watercolors, marking the beginning of Indian easel painting.

1918 ◆ Native American church established
Followers of the Peyote religion formed the Native American church in order to prevent U.S. courts and law officers from discriminating against their beliefs and ceremonies. *(Also see entries dated 1870-90: Peyote religion; and April 17, 1990: Oregon v. Smith.)*

1919 ◆ Maria Montoya Martinez, American Indian Artist
Probably the best known American Indian artist of the twentieth century, the San Ildefonso Pueblo potter Maria Martinez perfected many different styles of pottery, including the now-famous black-on-black ware she first developed with her husband around 1919. The ceramic renaissance Martinez and her family started had profound artistic and economic effects in the pueblos. *(Also see entry dated 1959: Maria Martinez presented the Jane Addanis Award.)*

1919 ◆ Mission Indian Federation formed
Indian children in California, as in other areas, were shipped off to government boarding schools in the late 1800s for the purpose of assimilation (becoming part of the mainstream society). One of the results was that they met many other Indian children from different tribes. Out of these relationships grew a sense of identity as Indians—not just as members of their own tribes. This sense of iden-

tity was sometimes called a pan-tribal consciousness (or, awareness of all tribes). This new awareness gave birth to pan-Indian (all-Indian) reform groups. The first such group to include California Indians was the Mission Indian Federation (MIF). The MIF worked for more independence for tribal governments, full civil rights for Indians, water rights, and the elimination of the the Dawes Act and the Bureau of Indian Affairs.

1919 ◆ U.S. Citizenship for Indian Veterans of World War I Act

Congress passed the U.S. Citizenship for Indian Veterans of World War I Act, granting U.S. citizenship to every American Indian who served in the armed services during World War I. *(Also see entry dated 1914-18: World War I.)*

c. 1920s ◆ American Indian Plains painting tradition

The American Indian Plains painting tradition came into existence with the "Kiowa Five," a group of painters from Oklahoma. The group mixed modern art techniques with traditional forms to create a distinctive Oklahoma style of painting.

1920 ◆ Forced enfranchisement in Canada

The Canadian government amended the Indian Act to allow for compulsory, or forced, enfranchisement, the process by which Indians would give up their tribal loyalties and become Canadian citizens. Only 250 Indians had voluntarily become enfranchised between 1857 and 1920. *(Also see entries dated 1857: Gradual Civilization Act in Canada; 1869: Gradual Enfranchisement Act; and 1876: Indian Act in Canada.)*

1920 ◆ Indian Defense League of America

The Indian Defense League of America (IDLA) was founded. The IDLA protested the disregard shown by the American and Canadian governments for Native treaty rights. IDLA protests included refusing to pay customs duties or use passports and resisting restrictions on movement between Canada and the United States.

1922 ◆ Navajo Business Council

After the Navajo settled on their reservation in the 1860s, the U.S. government ignored them until oil was discovered on their lands. Previously these lands had been considered useless. When oil was found, the government created the Navajo Business Council to grant oil and mineral leases in the name of the Navajo nation. Many of these leases were not favorable to the Navajo.

1923 ◆ Committee of One Hundred

Secretary of the Interior Hubert Work appointed the Committee of One Hundred to investigate American Indian policies and to make recommendations. The committee was formed as the result of pressure applied by reformers. The committee recommended increasing funds for health care, public education, scholarships, and court rulings on Indian land claims.

May 1923 ✦ American Indian Defense Association

The American Indian Defense Association (AIDA) was formed. The AIDA was different from other "Friends of the Indian" groups because it favored an end to land allotment and called for Indian cultural and religious freedom. AIDA also sought federal protection of Indian property and water rights, recognition of tribal claims, and improvement of Indian health standards and medical and educational services.

1924 ✦ Pueblo Land Act

When the United States took over the American Southwest in 1848 after the Mexican-American War the Pueblo, as Mexican citizens, were automatically granted U.S. citizenship. As U.S. citizens, the Pueblo did not receive the rights and protections granted to Indians as independent nations by the federal government. As a result, much Pueblo land, which was the finest farmland in the Southwest, was lost.

The Pueblo asked for, and then sued for, Indian status, which they gained in 1916. Meanwhile, they had lost some of their best lands as well as important religious sites. The All Indian Pueblo Council (a loose federation, or grouping, of Pueblo representatives) organized delegates from all the pueblos in an effort to regain their land. The resulting Pueblo Lands Act of 1924 restored Pueblo lands, but the battle was not over. Today the Pueblo fight hard to obtain and keep their water rights. Their lands are secure, but useless without water. *(Also see entry dated December 15, 1970: Taos Land Bill.)*

June 2, 1924 ✦ Indians granted U.S. citizenship

All Indians were granted U.S. citizenship. This change was brought about by the services Indian soldiers performed during the First World War and pressure applied by the Alaska Native Brotherhood. The act did not take away rights that Indians had by treaty or by the Constitution. It allowed them to vote in federal elections, but some states, such as New Mexico, prohibited Indians from voting in state elections. *(Also see entry dated 1914-18: World War I.)*

October 15, 1925 ✦ *The Vanishing American* premiered

The motion picture *The Vanishing American* was shown for the first time. The story of corruption and mismanagement on a modern-day reservation was based upon the writing of author Zane Grey.

1927 ✦ *Cogewea, the Halfblood* published

The first novel by an American Indian woman was *Cogewea, the Halfblood* by Mourning Dove. It was about a young Native American woman trying to decide whether to marry a non-Native or a half-Native man. She finally chose the man with Indian blood and affirmed her culture. The themes of being caught between two worlds and having to choose, and the problems faced by people of mixed heritage in American society, were taken up by other writers throughout the 1900s.

1928 ✦ Charles Curtis elected vice president

Charles Curtis of Kansas, a Kaw Indian and a U.S. senator for 25 years, was elected vice president of the United States to serve with President Herbert Hoover (1929-33). *(Also see entry dated 1906: Charles Curtis elected to Senate.)*

1928 ✦ Meriam Report

Multimillionaire John D. Rockefeller, Jr., hired Lewis Meriam to investigate the status of Indian economies, health, and education, and the federal administration of Indian affairs. Meriam published *The Problem of Indian Administration,* which listed the results of his study. The study described the terrible conditions under which Indians were forced to live. Meriam's report listed problems with Indian health care, education, poverty, malnutrition, and land ownership. The report urged the U.S. government to increase funding in all of these areas.

The Meriam Report section on the education of Native Americans described Indian boarding schools as deplorable. Many problems were found, including widespread illness, poor living conditions, and low teacher salaries. The report also criticized the Uniform Course of Study, which dictated that all Indian children should study the same things at the same time of year. In addition, the skills that were taught often did not prepare students for the job market.

Changes were made in the 1930s. Some of the boarding schools were closed. The Uniform Course of Study was gradually replaced with courses that were related to the cultures and traditions of the Native children. Bilingual books were used, and teachers were given training in order to promote bilingual education.

The report stated that poverty among Indians in the United States had three main causes:

1) The destruction of the Indians' traditional culture and economy.

2) The fundamental differences between Native American social systems and the U.S. economic system.

3) Past policies of the U.S. government.

Although the government set out to provide the food, clothing, education, and medicine they had promised to the conquered Indian nations, the government's management of Indian affairs often had the ulterior purpose of acquiring Indian land and natural resources for settlers. Impoverishment and inadequate means of supporting themselves caused Indians to become dependent on the government. Because of this economic dependence, the Bureau of Indian Affairs grew into a powerful force on reservations, according to the report.

1929-41 ◆ The Great Depression
The Great Depression (a period when the U.S. economy was weak and many people found themselves out of work) forced many Indian farmers and ranchers out of business. President Franklin D. Roosevelt designed programs such as the Works Progress Administration (WPA) to help people who could not find jobs. Roosevelt's "New Deal" programs helped many Indians, as well as non-Indians, through this difficult period.

1932 ◆ *Black Elk Speaks* published
"As told to" stories formed a special category of American Indian autobiography. These were Native life stories written with the help of others. In one of the most famous "as told to" biographies, *Black Elk Speaks,* writer John G. Neihardt presented the words of the Oglala Sioux warrior and medicine man with his own poetic understanding of Black Elk's vision.

Black Elk witnessed the Battle of Little Bighorn as a boy of 13. Many years later he experienced the massacre of Indians at Wounded Knee. Throughout his life his people were pushed into smaller and more regulated living areas. *Black Elk Speaks* tells of these events, but Black Elk's real intent was to express the meaning of all life that had been presented to him in several visions.

Many feel that *Black Elk Speaks* ranks among the most important holy books of the world. Swiss psychologist Carl Jung saw in it many similarities to the life stories of other religious figures. Jung's interest in the book helped it to be republished in 1959. Writer Vine Deloria, Jr., called *Black Elks Speaks* a "veritable Indian Bible" for youth of the 1960s and 1970s because it showed the beauty and value in traditional Native American religion.

1932-37 ◆ Santa Fe Studio style
When artist Dorothy Dunn began teaching art at the Santa Fe Indian School, the Santa Fe Studio style of painting was launched. Similar to the Oklahoma style, the Santa Fe Studio painters used flatly laid color fields and strong definition of lines, often with Pueblo or Navajo traditions as subjects for their art.

INDIANS IN MOVIES

In the 1930s, many "B Westerns" were made. These were low-budget cowboy pictures with simple "good guy vs. bad guy" plots. Because they were low-budget, costly scenes of Indian attacks or buffalo stampedes were used over and over again. Non-Indians in makeup were hired as extras.

By the mid-1930s, the cowboy became the benevolent hero of the movies, as he drove Indians from the Plains and made the frontier safe for settlers. *Stagecoach* (1939) showed Apaches being mowed down like blades of grass. This and many other Westerns that cast Indians as unwelcome aliens in their own land left an indelible mark on the American mind.

1933-50 ✦ John Collier and the crusade for Indian reform

John Collier, longtime director of the American Indian Defense Association and a social crusader for Indian rights, was appointed commissioner of Indian affairs by President Franklin D. Roosevelt. Under his leadership the administration began a program known as the "Indian New Deal," which set out to strengthen unique Indian cultures by fostering tribal government and Indian arts and crafts as well as by preserving valuable tribal artifacts and customs.

The Johnson-O'Malley Act was an important part of the "Indian New Deal." The act allowed the federal government to contract with states and territories to provide services for Indians, including health care, social welfare, and education. The commissioner of Indian affairs ordered the Indian Service to hire more Indians and to cease interference with Native American spiritual beliefs, ceremonies, and traditions. *(Also see entry dated 1934: Indian Reorganization Act.)*

As part of the New Deal of the Roosevelt Administration, American Indians joined the Works Progress Administration (WPA), the Public Works Administration (PWA), and the Civilian Conservation Corps (CCC). While participating in such programs as the CCC, Indian families were introduced to modern farming, ranching, and forestry techniques and were taught English and basic mathematics.

1934 ✦ Indian Reorganization Act

Realizing how destructive allotment was to Indian communities, the U.S. Congress passed the Indian Reorganization Act (IRA). The IRA ended allotment and restored some lands to the tribes. The IRA also encouraged tribes to govern themselves and set up tribal economic corporations. Even so, tribal governments did not gain enough power over their money and lands to become truly self-governing and often found the government overruling their decisions.

The IRA also led to increased activism on the reservations. Because the government provided more money to the reservations, Native Americans were able to take a new look at their situation and act together to try to correct it. Tribes had to decide whether or not to support the act, which brought land, money, and certain rights, but also some questionable new programs, to reservations. During this time, the government's Bureau of Indian Affairs interfered with self-government on several reservations and became a target of tribal protest. *(Also see entry dated 1933-50: John Collier and the crusade for Indian reform.)*

1934-41 ✦ Seneca Arts Project

With funding provided by New Deal programs like the Temporary Emergency Relief Administration (TERA) and the Works Progress Administration (WPA), the Seneca Arts Project led to the creation of over 5,000 works of art at the

Tonawanda and Cattaraugus Seneca Indian reservations. Both "traditional" and "nontraditional" art forms were produced, including face masks, bowls, spoons, cradleboards, moose hair and porcupine quillwork, silver jewelry, and baskets, as well as paintings and sculptures.

1935 ✦ Health care in Canada

In the case of *Dreaver* v. *Regina,* the Exchequer Court of Canada ruled that the "medicine chest" clause of Treaty 6 meant that Indians covered by this treaty should be given free medicines, drugs, and medical supplies. Indians had long argued that this was what the "medicine chest" clauses in all 11 treaties meant, but the Canadian government had denied that claim.

August 15, 1935 ✦ Will Rogers died

Will Rogers, part Cherokee, died in a plane crash near Point Barrow, Alaska. Rogers attracted media attention in the 1920s as cowboy, writer, actor, entertainer, and unique humorist, gaining considerable fame for his witty, homespun commentaries on politics and American life. He published widely read books, including *The Cowboy Philosopher on Prohibition* (1919) and *Will Rogers's Political Follies* (1929).

Hopi woman making pottery in Orabai village.

1936 ✦ Indian Actors Association

The Indian Actors Association was formed to provide more opportunities and better benefits for its Native American members. The group worked closely with the movies' central casting offices to encourage studios to hire Indians as actors and technical advisers.

August 27, 1936 ✦ Indian Arts and Crafts Board

The U.S. Congress created the Indian Arts and Crafts Board. This new government agency was designed to develop Indian arts and crafts and create a market for such products. It was hoped that the sale of arts and crafts would improve the economic welfare of Indian tribes.

1938 ✦ Hopi split over Indian Reorganization Act

The Hopi tribe split over their reaction to the Indian Reorganization Act (IRA). Although the IRA was meant to give Indian communities more control, many

Hopi rejected it because it did not fit their traditional way of life. They wanted a Hopi government, based on traditional Hopi customs and religion.

Conservative Hopi (those who wished to save, or "conserve," traditional ways) were some of the most active nationalist groups in the United States. During the next several years they appealed to organizations such as the United Nations for justice over broken treaty agreements and for recognition of their independence. Other Hopi, however, were willing to live under an IRA government and to accept some Western ways along with their Indian traditions. *(Also see entry dated 1934: Indian Reorganization Act.)*

1938 ✦ "Rules of 1938"

The Navajo rejected the Indian Reorganization Act (IRA), which would have given them a federally structured tribal government and constitution. Instead, they held their own constitutional convention, with the federal government's permission. The Navajo wrote a constitution which would give them independence from the Bureau of Indian Affairs (BIA).

The U.S. government rejected this plan and instead formed a new Navajo Business Council. This council was composed of 74 elected Navajo members and became known as the "Rules of 1938." It was the basis for the present Navajo Tribal Council.

During the late 1930s an extreme drought made the central and southern United States so dry the affected area was called the "dust bowl." At this time, the U.S. government decided that the Navajo were raising too many sheep and that their grazing would cause soil erosion, by stripping plant cover off topsoil, which would then dry out and blow away. Agents of the Agricultural Department killed tens of thousands of Navajo sheep. For several decades after this, relations between the Navajo and the U.S. government were hostile. *(Also see entry dated 1934: Indian Reorganization Act.)*

March 1938 ✦ *The Lone Ranger* released

Republic Pictures released *The Lone Ranger,* a 15-episode series about the adventures of a mysterious masked rider and his Indian companion, Tonto. From 1949 to 1957, ABC aired *The Lone Ranger* television series featuring Jay Silverheels (Mohawk) as Tonto. *(Also see entry dated July 21, 1979: Jay Silverheels' star.)*

1940s ✦ "Oklahoma" style of painting

Plains artists as far north as the Canadian prairies painted in what was sometimes called the "Oklahoma" style. These works revealed a longing for traditional culture with subjects like buffalo hunts and brilliantly costumed warriors doing ceremonial dances.

The President of the United States of America

Presents this

CERTIFICATE OF APPRECIATION

To

'The Navajo Code Talkers

in recognition of their dedicated service to America during World War II. Their unique achievements constitute a proud chapter in the history of the United States Marine Corps; their patriotism, resourcefulness, and courage have earned them the gratitude of all Americans.

The White House
Washington, D.C., December 1981

Ronald Reagan

1941-45 ◆ World War II and the Navajo Code Talkers

On December 7, 1941, the United States entered World War II. More than 25,000 Indian men and women joined the services and were honored with 71 Air Medals, 51 Silver Stars, 47 Bronze Stars, 34 Distinguished Flying Crosses, and 2 Congressional Medals of Honor. Those who remained home participated in the war effort through defense work, the purchasing of war bonds, blood drives, and collection of rubber, paper, and metal. In all, about 70,000 Indian men and women left the reservations to enter military service or the defense industries.

A group of Navajo had a special mission. They developed a code based on

In 1981 U.S. President Ronald Reagan recognized Navajo Code Talkers for their dedicated service during World War II.

Ira Hayes, Pima, was one of six marines to raise the American flag on the summit of Mount Suribachi on Iwo Jima, then held by the Japanese.

the Navajo language but constructed it in a way that even a Navajo speaker could not break it without knowing how it operated. The Japanese were never able to break the code. The Navajo Code Talkers probably saved the lives of thousands of U.S. soldiers.

Up to 6,000 Canadian Indians volunteered for service in World War II. Their status as noncitizens made them ineligible for the draft or for certain veterans' benefits. Their war effort included the construction of weather stations and military airfields.

July 18, 1942 ✦ Iroquois declared war

The Six Nations declared war on the Axis powers (Germany, Italy, and Japan). Claiming its right as an independent sovereign nation, the Iroquois League did not recognize the declaration of war by the U.S. government.

1944 ✦ Activisim after World War II

World War II stimulated a new group of Native American leaders, veterans who were not satisfied with the situation of Indians in the United States. After fighting and risking their lives for their country, they began to feel more entitled to society's rewards. The new leaders became more vocal in demanding greater self-determination and control over reservation resources. Native leaders also wanted rights equal to other citizens' and demanded that Congress repeal unfair laws. Tribal leaders met to form the National Congress of American Indians, a group dedicated to guarding Indian rights and preserving Native culture, reservations, and tribal lands.

Indian activism in the years after World War II was aimed mainly at projects that threatened Indian lands and sacred areas. The Iroquois resisted several water projects that affected their lands. These included Mohawk and Tuscarora protests against the St. Lawrence Seaway project in New York in the 1950s and 1960s. During this period the Iroquois protested treaty violations each year by demonstrating at the United Nations in New York. They wore traditional ceremonial clothing and used the media to capture public interest in their cause.

1944 ✦ William Stigler elected to U.S. Congress

William Stigler (Choctaw) was elected to the U.S. Congress from Oklahoma, and served in the 78th to 82d Congresses. He served as a city attorney from 1920 to 1924 and became a state senator in 1924, serving until 1932. Stigler died on August 21, 1952.

1945 ◆ Ira Hayes, Indian war hero

A full-blooded member of the Pima tribe, Ira Hayes was probably the most famous Indian soldier of World War II. He joined the marines in 1942 and in 1945 landed as part of the Fifth Marine Division assault troops on Iwo Jima, an island in the South Pacific held by the Japanese. There Hayes was one of six marines who raised the U.S. flag on the summit of Mount Suribachi under heavy enemy fire. An Associated Press photographer captured the moment on film, and it became one of the most inspiring war photographs ever taken. The famous bronze Marine monument in Washington, D.C., commemorating the battle of Iwo Jima, was based on this image.

1945 ◆ Iroquois sought membership in United Nations

The Iroquois of the Six Nations Reservation sent a delegation to the newly formed United Nations in San Francisco seeking membership. The application, however, was denied.

1946 ◆ Indian Claims Commission

By 1934 Native Americans owned only 48 million acres of land, and a great deal of this was in uninhabitable desert. Native peoples had lost over 98 percent of their lands. The Indian Lands Commission (ICC) was created to decide land claims filed by Indian nations. Many tribes expected the ICC to return lost lands, but the ICC chose to award money instead. This angered Native Americans, particularly in light of the ICC's policy of awarding money based on the value of the land at the time it was lost. Often this was not more than $1.25 per acre!

1947 ◆ *Smoke Signals* published

Marie Potts, a Maidu, created an intertribal newspaper, *Smoke Signals*; it was one of the earliest modern publications serving reservation and urban Indian populations in California. *Smoke Signals* sought to inform California Indians of current issues and events which specifically affected them. The publication also strove to promote intertribal cooperation, its motto being "In Unity There Is Strength."

June 3, 1948 ◆ Crazy Horse Monument dedicated

Five American Indian survivors of the Battle of the Little Bighorn were among participants in the dedication of the Crazy Horse monument in South Dakota. The monument was begun by sculptor Korczak Ziolkowski and will be completed with the help of contributions from interested private individuals and groups. The monument, which would take up an entire mountain top and be visible from all directions, was part of a plan that included a research center, a medical school for Indians, and other development projects.

1949 ♦ Hoover Commission

The Hoover Commission, led by former president Herbert Hoover, recommended that the federal government remove itself from responsibility for Indian affairs. Many congressional leaders supported this plan because they wanted to take advantage of the many natural resources, including timber, oil, gas, uranium, and water, that could be found on reservations.

1950 ♦ Sioux Sun Dance

The Sun Dance was revived among the Sioux.

June 20, 1951 ♦ A new Indian Act

A new Canadian Indian Act significantly reduced the power of the Indian Affairs Department but still listed assimilation as the aim of Indian policy. The new act made it easier for Indians to gain the right to vote and included provisions allowing Indian children to be placed in integrated provincial schools. It also removed the ban on potlatch and Sun Dance ceremonies. *(Also see entry dated 1876: Indian Act in Canada.)*

1952 ♦ Relocation

In the 1950s the U.S. government decided to end the "Indian problem" once and for all. Government officials decided to try to make Indians assimilate, or "blend in," with the rest of society, rather than keeping their own cultures. This policy meant moving Indians from reservations to cities. The government hoped Indians would find work in the cities and adopt an "American" life-style. Then, the government would be able to "terminate" the tribes and eliminate the reservations.

In 1952 the Bureau of Indian Affairs began a program to help Native Americans find jobs off the reservations. In 1956 the U.S. Congress passed a law that provided job skills training for Native Americans between the ages of 18 and 35. They would be given money to support themselves for six months while they were in training. By 1960 about 35,000 Native Americans had relocated, but one-third of those returned home to the reservations.

1953 ♦ First Miss Indian America

Arlene Wesley James, a Yakima from Washington, became the first Miss Indian America as the result of winning the featured event at the annual All American Indian Days celebration at Sheridan, Wyoming. Miss James traveled widely to represent the American Indian people as goodwill ambassador at many national and international events.

1954-62 ✦ Termination policy

The U.S. Congress began its policy of "termination" in 1953. Several tribes were terminated, meaning they lost their status and power as nations. Congress also passed a law that gave states and local governments control over tribal members. These actions took away the tribes' authority to govern themselves. Under the policy of termination, Indians were to lose their special privileges and be treated just the same as any other U.S. citizens. *(Also see entry dated 1965: Self-Determination Policy.)*

Termination was devastating for most tribes, who could barely survive as a community even with recognized tribal status. Without a trust relationship with the U.S. government (a relationship in which the government acts in the "best interests" of Native Americans; the government, in fact, owns Native American lands "in trust," and tribes are given use of it) and the rights they had been granted by law and treaty, most of these groups faced extreme poverty and the threat of loss of their community.

By 1961 the U.S. government began to realize that termination policies were causing damage to Native Americans. The government stated that terminating tribes hurt Indian morale and made the Native people angry or apathetic (not willing to make an effort). The statement went on to say that these reactions limited Native Americans' willingness to go along with other federal Indian programs.

1955 ✦ Indian Health Service

Responsibility for Indian health care was transferred to the Indian Health Service (IHS). The IHS operated hospitals, health centers, health stations, clinics, and community service centers.

February 1, 1958 ✦ Canada's first Indian senator

Kainai (Blood) James Gladstone was appointed as Canada's first Indian senator. Gladstone represented the province of Alberta.

June 12, 1958 ✦ Leo Johnson entered Air Force Academy

Leo Johnson of Fairfax, Oklahoma, entered the Air Force Academy in Colorado Springs, Colorado, becoming the first Indian to enter that select body of young Americans. He graduated and was commissioned as an officer in the Air Force on June 6, 1962. Johnson attained the rank of captain and became a pilot. In his career, Captain Johnson received seven Air Medals and the Air Force Commendation Medal.

1959 ✦ Maria Martinez received the Jane Addanis Award

Maria Martinez, Pueblo potter, was given the Jane Addanis Award by Rockford College, Rockford, Illinois, one of the highest honors ever granted to an Amer-

Maria Martinez,
potter of San
Ildefonso Pueblo,
New Mexico, and
her blackware
designs, 1940s.

ican woman artist. The award was given in recognition of Martinez's achievements as a potter. *(Also see entry dated 1919: Maria Montoya Martinez, American Indian artist.)*

1959 ✦ Navajo court system

The Navajo adopted a court system modeled after the U.S. legal system. The Navajo did not want the states of New Mexico and Arizona to extend their court systems onto the reservation, so they established their own courts, applying their own ideas of justice.

The Navajo often settled problems in a traditional manner, rather than by following U.S. law. For example, while many U.S. courts use the law to find one party right or wrong, many Navajo courts try to reconcile disputes between people. Resolution of conflict is a long-standing tradition in Navajo culture. During the 1970s the Navajo court system gained in power and respect, along with the Navajo government—the largest tribal government organization in Native North America.

March 31, 1960 ✦ Canadian Indians given the vote

A law giving status Indians in Canada the right to vote in the next Canadian federal election was approved by the queen of England. Some Indians protested against the change, claiming that it would take away their special rights and status as independent peoples.

December 1960 ✦ Ute seceded

A group of Ute Indians in Utah seceded (withdrew) from the United States in protest of government control over their land and mineral holdings. Although the Utes did not succeed in forming a separate nation, they did draw public attention to their cause.

1961 ✦ Chicago Indian Conference

Representatives from 90 tribes met in Chicago to oppose the policy of termination. The group emphasized additional academic training for Indian children, increased job training, improved housing on reservations, better medical facilities, access to loans for economic development, and increased efforts to develop industry and employment on the reservations.

1961 ✦ National Indian Youth Council

The African American Civil Rights movement of the early 1960s sparked widespread reform in the United States. Native American communities responded to the national movement with increased activism. The National Indian Youth Council was formed and challenged the more established Indian representatives such as the Christian churches, the National Congress of American Indians, and the Indian Rights Association. The council was in favor of a more activist and nationwide strategy for solving Indian problems, focusing attention during the 1960s on issues of education and discrimination and criticizing congressional leaders and the Bureau of Indian Affairs bureaucracy.

1962 ✦ Indian voting rights in New Mexico

The federal government forced New Mexico to allow its large Indian population to vote in state and local elections.

1962 ✦ Institute of American Indian Art

The Institute of American Indian Art (IAIA) was founded in Santa Fe, New Mexico. Students at the IAIA were given both traditional and modernist instruction, but as time passed the institute came to represent more modern American Indian art. Many Indians criticized the institute, saying that it should support only traditional Indian art.

December 1962 ✦ National Indian Council

The National Indian Council was formed as the first truly national Indian organization in Canada. Though it sought to represent status Indians (members of the 633 bands across Canada registered with the government) and non-status Indians (Indians who had lost the right to be registered, usually because of marriage to a non-Indian), most of its members were non-status Indians and Métis. By this time, the term "Métis" was used by many people to denote any person of mixed European and Indian ancestry, although the definition remains controversial. *(Also see entry dated February 1968: National Indian Council split.)*

1963 ✦ Annie Dodge Wauneka received Medal of Freedom

Annie Dodge Wauneka, the first woman to serve on the Navajo tribal council, was presented with the Medal of Freedom Award by President John F. Kennedy, only days before his assassination. This award was the country's highest peacetime honor, given to persons who had made outstanding contributions to the national interest or security or world peace, or who had otherwise made substantial contributions in public or private endeavors.

SNOWMOBILES REPLACED DOGSLEDS

The introduction of the small snowmobile in the North dramatically altered the lives of the Inuit and northern Indians. Although early snowmobiles were expensive, heavy, and prone to breakdowns, they were faster and carried larger loads than dog teams. The snowmobile made it easier for trappers to live in a single village all year, since they could now quickly travel long distances to get to hunting and fishing areas. Before snowmobiles, the Inuit and northern Indians lived in different locations in winter and summer to take advantage of seasonal hunting, fishing, and wild plant resources. With the development of more reliable machines, dogsleds were almost completely replaced by snowmobiles.

1963 ✦ Native American Movement began

The Native American Movement (NAM) was begun. NAM was designed to create sentiments of unity among persons of Native blood, especially Indians and Mexican Americans, in both North and South America. NAM promoted establishment of American Indian and Mexican American universities and pride in Indian descent. NAM also supported the use of the term "Native American" in place of "Indian."

December 1963 ✦ American Indian Arts Center

The American Indian Arts Center opened in New York City. Its purpose was to develop a broader appreciation and market for Indian and Eskimo craftsmanship and to display the high standards of Indian workmanship and the excellence of American Native art.

1964 ✦ American Indian Historical Society

The American Indian Historical Society was formed. The new group was dedicated to historical research and teaching about Native Americans. The society began publishing *The Indian Historian,* a journal that presented articles on Indian history from an Indian point of view.

1964 ✦ Native American museum

The first tribally controlled museum was established by the Cahuilla on the Morongo Indian Reservation in California.

October 14, 1964 ✦ Billy Mills won Olympic Gold Medal

Billy Mills, a Sioux from South Dakota, won the 10,000-meter run at the Olympic Games in Tokyo, Japan, in the world record time of 28 minutes and 24.04 seconds. This was the first time that an American had won a distance race in the Olympics. His victory is still considered one of the greatest athletic upsets of all time.

1964-66 ✦ Indian Community Action Programs

President Lyndon B. Johnson's Great Society legislation for fighting poverty was implemented with the creation of the Office of Economic Opportunity (OEO). The Bureau of Indian Affairs (BIA) wanted to administer Indian antipoverty funds, but the OEO, suspicious of past BIA management of Indian affairs, delivered antipoverty funds directly to the tribal governments. For the first time, most Indian tribal governments gained direct access to federal funds that were not administered by BIA officials. During the late 1960s and 1970s many tribal governments rapidly expanded in personnel, budget, and programs administered.

Mid-1960s ✦ Buffy Sainte-Marie

Buffy Sainte-Marie, a Cree composer and singer, had numerous hit singles, including "Universal Soldier" and "Until It's Time for You to Go." She became internationally known for both her folksinging and her songwriting talents. In addition to her antiwar ballads, Sainte-Marie also wrote songs about Native identity and injustices committed against American Indian peoples. Sainte-Marie was an active supporter of the Indian occupiers of Alcatraz Island in 1969, giving many benefit concerts to raise money for their efforts. In the early 1970s, she became a regular member on the PBS series *Sesame Street,* where she sought to dispel misconceptions and stereotypes about American Indians and to provide a positive role model to Indian and non-Indian youth. She was the founder of the Native North American Women's Association, a group sponsoring theater, arts, and education projects, and the Nihewan Foundation, a law school scholarship funded by her own concert performances.

Billy Mills at the 1964 Olympic Games.

1965 ✦ Self-Determination Policy

By this time the policy of termination had been ended. The U.S. government began a new policy, called the Self-Determination policy. Federal aid to reservations would now be given directly to the Indian tribes and not funneled through the Bureau of Indian Affairs.

Self-government for Indian tribes was now supported by the U.S. government, and a number of laws were passed to support Indian sovereignty. However, federal, state, and local governments still exerted control over reservations, and often interfered with the effective functioning of tribal governments. Some Native Americans felt this conflict prevented tribes from moving forward. *(Also see entry dated 1954-62: Termination policy.)*

Spring 1966 ✦ Rough Rock Demonstration School

The Navajo established the Rough Rock Demonstration School, the first school in modern times to be operated by a tribe. The founding of the school came about after statistics showed that more than half of all reservation school students failed to complete their high school education. Studies showed that discrimination and ignorance of Indian culture on the part of teachers were major causes of the poor results in these schools. The Navajo hoped that by running their own school, where Navajo was the primary language used, they would be able to reverse the dropout rate and improve the education of their children.

April 30, 1966 ✦ Second Native American appointed as Bureau of Indian Affairs commissioner

The U.S. Senate confirmed (approved) the appointment of Robert LaFollette Bennett (Oneida) as the Bureau of Indian Affairs commissioner. Bennett was only the second Indian ever appointed to lead this agency, which had control over national Indian policy. *(Also see entry dated 1869-71: First Native American appointed as commissioner of Indian Affairs.)*

October 1966 ✦ Hawthorn Report

The first volume of *A Survey of the Contemporary Indians of Canada* (Hawthorn Report) was released. The report criticized Canadian Indian policy, noting that Natives were an economically, socially, and politically disadvantaged group in Canadian society. In addition to the normal rights and duties of citizenship, according to the report, Indians possessed certain additional rights as charter members of the Canadian community. Indian leaders supported the report.

1967 ✦ Alaska Federation of Natives formed

The influx of people and money to Alaska in the twentieth century caused conflict among Native peoples, and they soon formed an opposition movement. Often they were not consulted when major projects were planned on or near their lands. For example, the U.S. Atomic Energy Commission gave permission to use 1,600 square miles around Point Hope (an Inuit village) for a nuclear explosion. This explosion was to create a deep water port on the northwestern coast of Alaska.

Alaska Natives organized to prevent more of these situations and to protect their rights. By 1967 they had formed 12 regional associations to pursue land claims. The regional leaders then formed the Alaska Federation of Natives (AFN). The purpose of the AFN was to protect Native rights, inform the public about Native issues, preserve Native culture and values, and try to settle land claims.

February 1968 ✦ National Indian Council split

The National Indian Council separated into the National Indian Brotherhood (NIB) and the Canadian Métis Society. The NIB would seek to protect benefits that status Indians (members of the 633 Canadian Indian bands registered with the government) enjoyed under treaties and the Indian Act. The Canadian Métis Society would seek to protect the aboriginal rights of Métis (those of mixed

Native and non-Native ancestry) and non-status Indians (those Native people who had lost the right to be registered as Indians with the government). *(Also see entry dated December 1962: National Indian Council.)*

March 6, 1968 ✦ "The Forgotten American"
President Lyndon B. Johnson delivered his "Special Message to Congress on the Problem of the American Indian: The Forgotten American." Johnson outlined three goals in his message: (1) "A standard of living for the Indian equal to that of the country as a whole"; (2) "Freedom of choice: an opportunity to remain in their homelands, if they choose, without surrendering their dignity; and opportunity to move to towns and cities of America, if they choose, equipped with the skills to live in equality and dignity"; and (3) "Full participation in the life of modern America, with a full share of economic opportunity and social justice."

March 6, 1968 ✦ National Council on Indian Opportunity established
President Johnson established the National Council on Indian Opportunity. The Council's purposes were as follows:

1) to encourage the complete application of federal programs designed to aid Indians;
2) to encourage interagency cooperation in the implementation of these programs;
3) to assess the effect of these programs
4) to suggest ways in which these programs could be improved.

Many Indian groups were suspicious of the Council's activities. They worried that the real aim of the government was to take away their rights.

April 11, 1968 ✦ American Indian Civil Rights Act
The U.S. Congress passed the American Indian Civil Rights Act. The Act guaranteed to members of reservations the same civil rights and liberties in relation to their tribal authorities that the U.S. Constitution guaranteed to all persons in relation to federal and state authorities. The act was meant to guarantee that the constitutional rights of individual American Indians could not be violated by any governing body, including the tribal government. Some tribal leaders, especially the Pueblo, worried about the act. Because many Native American cultures are oriented to community as opposed to individual well-being, some leaders felt it might interfere with the powers of traditional governments.

May 18, 1968 ✦ Navajo peace treaty celebrated
President Johnson signed a bill commemorating the federal government's treaty with the Navajo. The Navajo nation, the largest in the United States, inhabited a 16 million acre reservation located in Arizona, New Mexico, and Utah. In

Tear gas and news cameras at the Puyallup fishing rights protest, Tacoma, Washington, 1970.

terms of population and land, the Navajo Nation was larger than 26 independent countries in the world.

May 27, 1968 ✦ *Puyallup Tribe* v. *Department of Game*

The U.S. Supreme Court ruled in the case of *Puyallup Tribe* v. *Department of Game* that Washington State had the right to prohibit Indian net fishing for salmon in the interest of conservation. The case was important because it gave states the right to violate Indian fishing rights guaranteed in treaties. *(Also see entry dated 1974: "Fish-in" movement.)*

June 25, 1968 ✦ First Indian elected to Canadian House of Commons

Leonard Marchand, an Okanagan (Interior Salish) from British Columbia, became the first Indian elected to the House of Commons. He later became a member of the Canadian cabinet.

July 1968 ✦ American Indian Movement founded

The American Indian Movement (AIM) was founded in Minneapolis, Minnesota, by Dennis Banks, a member of the Ojibway (Chippewa) Nation, and Russell Means, a member of the Lakota (Sioux) Nation. AIM was formed to improve federal, state, and local social services to urban neighborhoods and to prevent the harassment of Indians by the local police. AIM became one of the leaders of the "Red Power" movement of the late 1960s and 1970s, a combination of the efforts of many Native American groups. Other founders of the movement included Clyde Bellecourt (Ojibway) and Mary Jane Wilson.

1969 ✦ First "new" totem pole raised

The first "new" totem pole was raised in the Haida village of Masset, British Columbia. Totem poles had been banned along with potlatches by the Canadian government in 1884.

Traditionally, totem poles were built when a chief claimed the name of one of his deceased ancestors. Totem poles were carved from cedar logs. A series of animal and human figures were stacked one on top the other; each represented an event in family history, particularly one with spiritual meaning.

1969 ✦ "Indian Education: A National Tragedy—A National Challenge"

"Indian Education: A National Tragedy—A National Challenge" was published. This report described Indian education as "disastrous." High absenteeism and dropout rates, academic failures, and negative self-esteem were cited as problems. The report said that these problems resulted from schooling that failed to understand or adapt to Native American cultures. The report recommended teaching Indian history, culture, and language and involving Indian parents in the education of their children.

1969 ✦ Native American Student Union

The Native American Student Union was formed in the San Francisco Bay area, bringing together Indian college students. Members of the Native American Student Union became deeply involved in the November occupation of Alcatraz Island. *(Also see entry dated November 20, 1969: Alcatraz Island occupied.)*

January 21, 1969 ✦ Navajo Community College opened

The Navajo Community College opened at Many Farms, Arizona. The college was the first tribally established and controlled community college.

Spring 1969 ✦ Native American Studies program created

A protest by the University of California, Berkeley campus, chapter of United Native Americans led to the creation of a Native American Studies program at the university. Plans were also developed for Native American Studies centers on other California college campuses.

Native American Studies (NAS) programs focused on preserving the culture and history of Native peoples and promoting an "Indian perspective" in many colleges and universities. Although NAS programs began in the United States, Native Studies programs can now be found in Canada, most of the American republics, and several European countries. Centers for native people in New Zealand, Australia, and Norway have also been created.

March 5, 1969 ✦ Office of Minority Business Enterprise formed

The Office of Minority Business Enterprise was formed by President Richard Nixon. The act's objective for Native Americans was to assist tribes in the economic development of their reservations, where more than half of all families lived in poverty and the unemployment rate ran as high as 90 percent.

March 23, 1969 ✦ Mohawks on trial

The trial of seven Mohawk Indians began. The Mohawks were arrested for demonstrating on the International Bridge in upstate New York between Canada and the United States. The demonstration was caused by a dispute over treaty rights concerning the Mohawks' ability to take goods across the border without paying any duties (taxes on trade). The Mohawk reservation was located on both sides of the U.S.-Canadian border and Indians were charged taxes for taking goods from one family members' house to another.

May 5, 1969 ✦ Native American's novel won Pulitzer Prize

N. Scott Momaday, a Cherokee and Kiowa writer, was awarded the Pulitzer Prize for his book *House Made of Dawn.* (The Pulitzer Prize is awarded to outstanding works of fiction and nonfiction.) Momaday's novel told the story of Abel, a young Indian from San Juan Pueblo who returned from service in World War II and found readjustment to his life difficult and painful. Although Abel no longer felt "at home" on the reservation, when he attempted to relocate to Los Angeles, he experienced prejudice and felt uncomfortable in the dominant urban society. Momaday was the first Native American awarded a Pulitzer since the prize was first awarded in 1917.

House Made of Dawn ushered in what literary critics have called a "Native American Renaissance." In the 25 years after the publication of Momaday's classic work, greater and greater numbers of American Indian writers found their way into print, many of them citing Momaday as an important influence in their lives and work.

June 25, 1969 ✦ "White Paper"

Jean Chrétien, Canada's minister of Indian affairs, released the federal government's White Paper (government policy paper), *Statement of the Government of Canada on Indian Policy, 1969.* The discussion paper argued that Indians' special legal status had hindered their social, economic, and political development. The government proposed legislation to end all legal and constitutional distinctions relating to Indians. The Indian Act and the Indian Affairs Department were to be abolished in about five years; reserves, held in trust by the government since before Canada's Confederation, would pass to Indian ownership. Thus, the federal and provincial governments would deal with Indians in the same way they dealt with any other Canadians. During the transitional period (until the changes were completed), the government proposed to give Indians aid to fight social and economic problems on reserves. The policy paper dismissed aboriginal land claims as "so general and undefined that it is not realistic to think of them as ... capable of remedy."

Indians and Indian organizations from across Canada began to unite in opposition. As early as June 26 Walter Deiter, leader of the National Indian Brotherhood, rejected the White Paper, saying that it ignored both the views Indians expressed during the government's consultations with them and the guarantees given Indians in treaties. Harold Cardinal, Cree leader of the Indian Association of Alberta, wrote *Unjust Society,* a denunciation of the White Paper. During the winter *Unjust Society* became a Canadian best-seller. *(Also see entry dated June 4, 1970: "Red Paper.")*

September 1969 ✦ Indian Employment Training Center
An employment training center for Indians of the northern Plains states was opened at Bismarck, North Dakota, by a corporation composed of the Indian tribes of that state. The United Tribes of North Dakota Development Corporation became the first center begun by Indians and having an Indian contractor.

October 1969 ✦ *AMERIND*
AMERIND, an organization founded to protect the rights and improve the working conditions of Indian federal government employees, was formed. Supported by the National Indian Youth Council, AMERIND was established to fight employment discrimination and end the "second-class treatment" of Indians working for the Bureau of Indian Affairs, U.S. Public Health Service, and other federal agencies serving Indian people.

October 12, 1969 ✦ Dartmouth College dropped Indian mascot
Dartmouth College, located in New Hampshire and originally established in 1769 to educate Indians, announced that it was dropping its use of an Indian mascot in response to student demands. Indian students claimed that having such a mascot was insulting to Indian people.

October 13, 1969 ✦ Ford Foundation Minority Fellowships
The Ford Foundation announced the establishment of a Minority Fellowship Program for minority students, including American Indians. The program's objective was to increase the number of minority scholars obtaining doctorates in a variety of fields. At this time few Indians entered and completed college, and even fewer went on to graduate school. Educators recognized that it would be difficult to improve educational services to Indian students if they had no appropriate role models.

November 1969 ✦ National Indian Education Association formed
The National Indian Education Association (NIEA) was formed with the objective of improving the quality of Indian education. The NIEA worked to promote

A view of Alcatraz Island soon after the occupation by American Indian students.

increased funding for Indian education and to provide creative programs and technical assistance to teachers.

November 20, 1969 ◆ Alcatraz Island occupied

In the early morning hours of November 20, 1969, 89 Native Americans landed on Alcatraz Island in San Francisco Bay in California. Alcatraz was formerly a U.S. penitentiary. The group, calling itself "Indians of All Tribes," claimed possession of the island by the "right of discovery." It justified its actions with an 1868 Sioux treaty that gave Indians the right to unused federal property on Indian land. The Indians of All Tribes planned to use the island as a center for Native American spiritual, educational, and cultural activity. Part of the statement the Indians of All Tribes gave to the press said:

> We, the native Americans, re-claim the land known as Alcatraz Island in the name of all American Indians by right of discovery.... We will purchase said Alcatraz for twenty-four dollars in glass beads and red cloth.... Our offer of $1.24 per acre is greater than the 47 cents per acre the white men are now paying the California Indians for their land.

Native Americans, numbering anywhere from 15 to 1,000, occupied Alcatraz for the next 19 months. Usually there were about 100 Native Americans on the island at a time. They came from many different tribes, including the Sioux, Navajo, Cherokee, Mohawk, Puyallup, Yakima, Hoopa, and Omaha. During the months of occupation the Indians held news conferences, pow-wows, and celebrations while they negotiated with federal officials. Those occupying Alcatraz had to deal with hardships as federal officials interfered with boats bringing in supplies and cut off the supply of water and electricity to the island. The occu-

"Declaration of the Return of Indian Land," set forth by Indians of All Tribes at Alcatraz, California.

pation was very peaceful and the Indians made the American public aware of their position. However, the government did not accept the Indians' offer to purchase the island.

1970s ◆ American Indian Press Association

The American Indian Press Association was founded. It worked to gather and distribute news and information to dozens of reservation and community newspapers across Indian Country.

Many tribal leaders shared a strong belief that the media—television, radio, films, and printed matter—formed a powerful tool that could help them achieve their goals. Some of these goals were to protect their lands and natural resources; improve tribal economies and businesses; develop housing, education, and health programs; and preserve their traditional culture.

1970s ◆ American Indian Theatre Ensemble

The American Indian Theatre Ensemble (later called the Native American Theatre Ensemble) was founded. It was the first professional acting company composed entirely of Indian performers. In the years that followed, more than a dozen other Native American theaters were established across the United States.

1970s ◆ Indian sit-ins and takeovers

The late 1960s and early 1970s saw an increase of Indian protests. These protests took the form of peaceful takeovers and sit-ins, much like those engaged in by members of the African American civil rights movement of the early 1960s. Many of the occupations included festive celebrations of Native culture and traditions.

The occupation of Alcatraz Island provided a clear plan of action for the Red Power movement, as the series of Native American protest activities during the 1960s and 1970s was called. A key goal was the recovery by nonviolent protest of unused federal property. An abandoned military base, Fort Lawton, in Washington, was invaded by a group called United Indians of All Tribes. Actress Jane Fonda and 13 Indians were arrested in the initial attempt to take the base. The group demanded that it be given to them for use as an Indian cultural center, and it was, after much struggle, in 1971.

In 1970 several offices of the Bureau of Indian Affairs were occupied in protest of its employment practices. In Colorado, an American Indian woman applying for a position as school counselor working with Indian children was turned down despite her qualifications for the job. Native American activists protested by taking over the BIA office in Denver. On July 7, 1971, Deganawida-Quetzalcoatl University (DQU) opened on an abandoned army communications base in Davis, California. The site for the school was seized in November 1970 by approximately 40 Indians. DQU was set up as an Indian-run university. *(Also see entry dated November 20, 1969: Alcatraz Island occupied.)*

1970s ✦ Navajo formed labor unions

As the Navajo began to work more in industry, they found racial discrimination in pay and in duties assigned. As a result they formed trade unions, which had been banned on the reservation. By the late 1970s almost all Navajo workers in private firms (as opposed to government workers) were members of labor unions. The higher wages resulting from unionized jobs, combined with traditional Native practices of sharing and generosity among family and clan, helped to raise the standard of living among the Navajo.

1970s ✦ Woodland School of artists

The Woodland School (or the Legend Painters) chose traditional subjects and styles but used nontraditional materials and techniques, such as acrylic paint on canvas. Ojibway painter Norval Morrisseau, the best known member of the school, painted brilliantly colored and often very large canvases using synthetic acrylic paints. Morrisseau's subject matter was taken from such differing sources as traditional Algonkian pictography, rock art, and the stained glass windows of his childhood Catholic church.

1970 ✦ American Indian Youth Council

Indian youth groups began to press for change and work for a "new look" for the "First Americans." Indian youth set out to accomplish change through the use of political power and activism. Because of the formal nature of treaty relations with the federal government, activist protests and demonstrations had not been considered an acceptable "Indian" option by older and sometimes more conservative Indians. Consequently, youth strategies, influenced by the African American civil rights movement of the 1960s, became more radical.

June 4, 1970 ✦ The "Red Paper"

Two hundred Indians from across Canada presented *Citizen Plus* (the "Red Paper") to Minister of Indian Affairs Jean Chrétien and Prime Minister Pierre Trudeau. This Indian response to the government's "White Paper" condemned the proposal to remove Indians' special status and to transfer responsibility for Indians to the provinces. The Red Paper demanded that the special status of Indians be preserved, that treaty obligations be kept, and that an Indian Claims Commission be formed with the power to settle land claims. Prime Minister Trudeau agreed to withdraw the White Paper after this protest. *(Also see entry dated June 25, 1969: "White Paper.")*

July 8, 1970 ✦ Policy of Indian Self-Determination

The federal policy of Indian self-determination was announced. President Richard Nixon delivered his message to Congress calling for the self-determination of Indian people without termination of federal services or status. This

Members of the Iroquois League protesting for their rights to cross U.S.-Canadian border in accordance with 1794 Jay's Treaty.

message formally brought the termination policy to an end and promoted the notion of self-determination as a way to "strengthen the Indian's sense of autonomy without threatening his sense of community." The new policy also stated that services provided to Native Americans were not charity, but rather obligations the federal government had incurred in exchange for Indian lands. "To terminate this relationship would be no more appropriate than to terminate the citizenship rights of any other American," the statement said.

President Nixon used the Zuni Pueblo as an example to all Indian communities seeking greater self-government. The Zuni did not want the government to run their affairs, so in the late 1960s they gained control of community programs previously run by the Bureau of Indian Affairs (BIA). The Zuni ran many of their programs more effectively than the BIA had done, with more participation of members of the community.

July 12, 1970 ✦ Iroquois Confederacy meeting

Two hundred members of the Iroquois Confederacy met in Geneva, New York, to discuss ways to regain political power lost to the state and federal governments. The Iroquois still claimed to be an independent nation and issued their own passports, something only countries could do.

The Iroquois have survived as a nation and they have struggled to maintain their ancient traditions. The Iroquois culture has had to change in order to support itself in modern America. Today, the Iroquois work in many professions in the American economy around them. They are ironworkers, steelworkers, teachers, business people, and artists. But Iroquois languages are still spoken and taught. At the Onondoga Reservation, the Great Law set forth by Deganawidah is still recited. The Longhouse religion started by the Seneca prophet Handsome Lake in the 1830s has been revived.

Handsome Lake and his followers also revived the traditional chief system of leadership, and today it is present on the Onondaga, Tuscarora, and Tonawanda Seneca reservations in New York. In the Iroquoian chieftainship system, clan mothers nominate the chiefs of their clans. Chiefs are initiated to office through an ancient ceremony. Great festivals with traditional readings and thanksgiving ceremonies are attended by many Iroquois from both cities and reservations. *(Also see entry dated 1799: Handsome Lake.)*

December 15, 1970 ✦ Taos Land Bill

President Richard Nixon signed the Taos Land Bill. The legislation returned to the Taos Pueblo the sacred area of Blue Lake and 55,000 surrounding acres of land. The Pueblo had struggled for 30 years for the return of this sacred land, which they considered the navel of the universe and the place where the Creator first created people. The people of Taos Pueblo now hold annual ceremonies at Blue Lake, which they believe ensures their well-being and prosperity. The return of Blue Lake gave other Indian peoples hope that they might be successful in regaining and protecting their sacred areas. *(Also see entry dated 1924: Pueblo Land Act.)*

1971 ✦ Alaska Native Claims Settlement Act

Conflicts arose in Alaska over ownership of lands and other rights, especially after oil was discovered soon after Alaska became a state in 1959. Oil companies wanted to build a pipeline across Native lands to carry oil south, Alaska Natives wanted their land, and conservationists wanted to preserve wilderness areas. To settle these conflicts, the Alaska Native Claims Settlement Act

(ANCSA) was signed into law on December 18, 1971. With this act, Alaska Natives gave up any claim to title to nine-tenths of Alaska. In return for this, they were given $962 million and clear title to 44 million acres of land.

ANCSA cleared the path for the construction of the pipeline. It also set aside millions of acres of public lands for parks and wilderness areas. The ANCSA also resulted in the formation of 12 regional corporations to be in charge of economic development and land use. It was assumed that these profit-making corporations would lead to an improved standard of living for Alaskan Natives. The act, however, remained controversial among Alaskan Natives, who feared it would destroy their traditional life-style centered on hunting and fishing.

1971 ◆ The Five Civilized Tribes
The Bureau of Indian Affairs established regulations for the direct election of the chiefs of the Five Civilized Tribes—the Cherokee, Chickasaw, Choctaw, Creek, and Seminole. The Bureau of Indian Affairs had been appointing the tribes' chiefs since the 1890s. The tribes viewed the return of control over their own electoral system as an important step in the renewal of their governments. *(Also see entry dated November 16, 1907: Five Civilized Tribes school systems closed.)*

1971 ◆ Native American Rights Fund created
The Native American Rights Fund was created. The organization's objectives were to pursue the legal protection of Indian lands, treaty rights, and individual rights and to develop tribal law.

February 19-20, 1971 ◆ National Tribal Chairman's Association
Tribal leaders from 50 reservations in 12 states met to create the National Tribal Chairman's Association. The tribal leaders were afraid that their power was being threatened by the young radicals who were participating in protests.

February 22, 1971 ◆ Dan George nominated for Oscar
The Academy of Motion Picture Arts and Sciences announced the nomination of Canadian Squamish actor Dan George for best actor in a supporting role. George portrayed the elderly medicine man, Old Lodge Skins, in *Little Big Man* (1971).

April 30, 1971 ◆ James Bay Hydroelectric Project
The Quebec government announced the James Bay Hydroelectric Project in northern Quebec. The Cree and Inuit tribes of the region, who viewed the project as a threat to their way of life, had not been consulted before this announce-

ment, although Quebec had agreed to do so in a 1912 agreement. The Indian groups, afraid that the building of dams would flood their lands, went to court to try to stop the project. Soon the Quebec government decided to negotiate with the Indian tribes. *(Also see entry dated November 11, 1975: James Bay and Northern Quebec Agreement.)*

May 15, 1971 ✦ Hopi strip-mining suit

The Native American Rights Fund filed suit in federal court on behalf of 62 members of the Hopi tribe to stop strip-mining on 100 square miles of the Hopi Reservation in northern Arizona. The religious leaders contended that Black Mesa was an area of sacred importance to Hopi religion and culture. The suit was part of a larger effort by other Indians and conservationists to stop the development of a major power producing grid in the Four Corners (where Colorado, New Mexico, Arizona, and Utah come together) area. The Hopi traditionalists' (supporters of customary or traditional ways, ideas, and actions) objective was to prevent the Peabody Company from mining coal for use in six proposed power plants.

June 6, 1971 ✦ First female Native American lawyer

Yvonne Knight, a member of the Ponca tribe of Oklahoma, was the first known American Indian woman to receive a jurist doctorate (law) degree.

June 6-7, 1971 ✦ Indians occupied Mount Rushmore

Forty Indians established a camp on top of the Mount Rushmore National Memorial. The group demanded that the federal government honor its 1868 treaty with the Sioux Nation, which provided that all lands west of the Missouri River would belong forever to the Sioux Nation. Police arrested 20 protestors for climbing the monument.

June 11, 1971 ✦ Alcatraz occupation ended

The 19-month takeover of Alcatraz Island ended with the removal by federal marshals of the last 15 Indian demonstrators occupying the former prison. *(Also see entry dated November 20, 1969: Alcatraz Island occupied.)*

September 16, 1971 ✦ Southwestern Indian Polytechnic Institute

Southwestern Indian Polytechnic Institute was dedicated in Albuquerque, New Mexico. The school would serve 700 Native American students from 64 tribes. It offered training in business management, clerical work, drafting, radio, electronics, commercial food preparation, telecommunications, television, engineering, and optical technology.

October 8, 1971 ✦ Multicultural policy in Canada

The Canadian government adopted a policy of multiculturalism under which grants would be given to ethnic minorities, including aboriginals (original inhabitants of the area), to encourage them to retain aspects of their cultures.

1972 ✦ *Bury My Heart at Wounded Knee*

Dee Brown's *Bury My Heart at Wounded Knee,* which became a best-seller, told the Native American side of the story of the settling of the American West.

1972 ✦ Indian Education Act

Until this time education beyond high school was seen as unnecessary for Native Americans by many U.S. policymakers, who felt Indians would benefit more from job training than academic pursuits. In the 1950s a few colleges established special programs to train teachers who might work on or near reservations. In 1963 the first college preparatory program for Native Americans was established at Haskell Institute in Oklahoma. Haskell became a junior college two years later.

The Indian Education Act, followed by additional legislation, began a shift in federal policy toward providing the opportunity for college education for Native Americans. The number of Indian students enrolled in college grew to be five times greater by the end of the 1970s than it had been in the early 1960s.

February 19, 1972 ✦ Chippewa rights upheld

The Chippewa, through a federal court order, regained their right to hunt, fish, trap, and gather wild rice according to tribal laws on their reservation. The court agreed that an 1855 treaty guaranteed these rights to the Chippewa.

March 7, 1972 ✦ National American Indian Council formed

Urban Indians formed the National American Indian Council. The council's mission was to work on behalf of urban Indians worldwide.

November 2-8, 1972 ✦ Trail of Broken Treaties

Five hundred Indians arrived in Washington, D.C., on a march called the Trail of Broken Treaties to protest the government's policies toward Indians. The leaders, mostly members of the American Indian Movement, brought with them a 20-point program. This program called for improved cultural and economic conditions for Indians, the return of Indian lands, and the reestablishment of treaty relations between tribes and the federal government. The protesters occupied the Bureau of Indian Affairs building. After almost a week of occupation, during which activists destroyed files, furniture, and Indian art, the government agreed to pay for the protesters' return trip home. The administration rejected the demands of the leaders of the Trail of Broken Treaties.

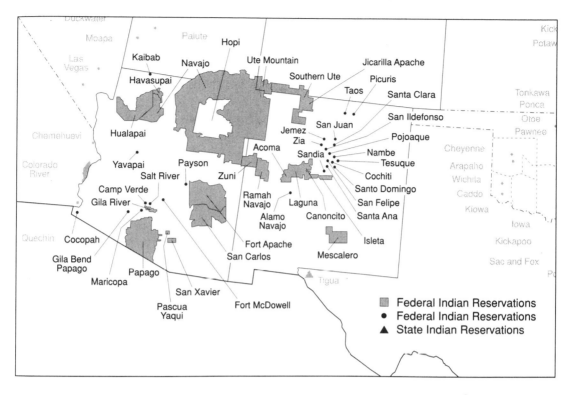

Duckwater
Moapa
Paiute
Hopi
Kick
Potaw

Las Vegas
Kaibab
Navajo
Ute Mountain
Jicarilla Apache

Havasupai
Southern Ute
Picuris
Tonkawa
Ponca

Taos
Santa Clara

Chemehuevi
Hualapai
San Ildefonso
Otoe
Pawnee

Jemez
Zia
San Juan
Pojoaque
Cheyenne

Colorado River
Acoma
Sandia
Nambe
Arapaho
Wichita

Yavapai
Payson
Zuni
Tesuque
Caddo

Salt River
Cochiti
Kiowa

Camp Verde
Gila River
Ramah Navajo
Laguna
Santo Domingo
San Felipe

Iowa

Quechin
Cocopah
Alamo Navajo
Canoncito
Santa Ana
Kickapoo

Gila Bend Papago
Fort Apache
San Carlos
Isleta
Sac and Fox

Maricopa
Papago
Mescalero

San Xavier
Fort McDowell
Tigua

Pascua Yaqui

■ Federal Indian Reservations
• Federal Indian Reservations
▲ State Indian Reservations

Contemporary southwestern tribes.

December 1972 ✦ "Indian Control of Indian Education"

The National Indian Brotherhood (NIB) presented "Indian Control of Indian Education," a statement that called for greater band (tribal) control of Indian education in Canada. The NIB statement called attention to the fact that Indians did not enjoy parental or local control over education—rights taken for granted by most Canadians. The Department of Indian Affairs supported the statement.

On May 24, 1973, the federal government announced that Indians would be given greater control of their education and that responsibility for Indian education would not be transferred to the provinces without consultation with Natives. The NIB welcomed the announcement.

1973 ✦ Hopi-Navajo Joint Use Area

During the nineteenth century, Navajo had begun to settle on Hopi lands, which brought about frequent clashes between the Navajo and Hopi. After growing conflict between the two nations, U.S. courts had created a Joint Use Area— 1.8 million acres to be shared between them. Only a portion of the Hopi reservation was held for the exclusive use of the Hopi. In 1973 clashes broke out between the Hopi and the Navajo over the Joint Use Area. In 1974 the U.S. Congress passed the Hopi and Navajo Relocation Act. The Joint Use Area was divided between the two nations, and $16 million compensation was provided to eight hundred Navajo families who were required to relocate. The Navajo were not happy with this settlement, and the Hopi refused to negotiate about the mandatory Navajo relocations.

February 27-May 8, 1973 ◆ Wounded Knee II

Wounded Knee II, the 1973 occupation of the Pine Ridge reservation in South Dakota, started with a dispute over the Oglala Sioux tribal chairman, Robert Wilson. Some tribe members felt Wilson was a puppet of the Bureau of Indian Affairs and wanted to impeach (remove) him. When Wilson and his administration began beatings and shootings to enforce "Wilson rule," Sioux traditionalists called in the American Indian Movement (AIM). Wilson's supporters and local authorities armed themselves against protesters, who were also armed, and a siege began that lasted ten weeks. Federal law enforcement officials, the Bureau of Indian Affairs, local citizens, celebrities, and national news media all became involved. Three hundred federal marshals and FBI agents surrounded the Indian protesters. The siege peaked when the two sides began firing on each other and two Native American men were shot and killed. The conflict ended soon after the shooting, when both sides agreed to a negotiated settlement, but violence and conflict continued on the Pine Ridge reservation. *(Also see entries dated September 16, 1974: AIM leaders released; and September 13, 1983: Dennis Banks surrendered.)*

March 27, 1973 ◆ Marlon Brando refused Oscar

Sacheen Littlefeather, wearing buckskin, a headband, and braids, refused the Oscar for best actor on Marlon Brando's behalf for his role in *The Godfather*. Standing in front of the large audience at the Academy Award presentation, Littlefeather explained that the veteran actor's decision was a result of "the treatment of Indians by the film industry, in television, in the movie reruns, and the recent happenings in Wounded Knee, South Dakota."

August 13, 1973 ◆ Office of Indian Rights created

The Office of Indian Rights was created within the Civil Rights Division of the Justice Department. The office was established to investigate and to protect individual Indian rights.

1974 ◆ "Fish-in" movement

In the African American civil rights movement of the 1960s, "sit-ins" were a popular form of protest against racist practices such as the refusal of restaurants to serve black Americans at the same counters as white Americans. Native American activists used "fish-ins" to protest the loss of their fishing rights in the Northwest.

In a 1957 Supreme Court case in Washington state, Robert Satiacum, a Puyallup and Yakima, was tried for fishing out of season. Many Native American spokespeople held that they were given the right to fish by treaty, and that the state of Washington had no power to determine the season for their fishing. The court's decision was split 4 to 4, but police continued to restrict fishing activities. And the Indian fishermen continued to cast their nets. National figures like comedian Dick Gregory and actor Marlon Brando supported the fishermen and brought national attention to the tribes' cause. Finally in 1974 the U.S. Supreme Court, in the case of *Department of Game of Washington* v. *Puyallup Tribe et al,* restored the Indian fishing rights, and the fish-in movement ended. The victory encouraged Red Power activists all over the country to continue to fight to regain Indian rights.

1974 ✦ Women of All Red Nations
A group of female American Indian Movement (AIM) activists formed the Women of All Red Nations (WARN). By organizing Native women in an untraditional political forum, the WARN founders felt that they could fulfill their traditional responsibilities to protect and ensure Native rights for all.

April 1974 ✦ Northern Flood Committee
Indian bands in northern Manitoba, Canada, formed the Northern Flood Committee to represent them in negotiations with the Manitoba government. The government promised to compensate them for any damage caused by hydroelectric developments planned for the province. In 1976 the project flooded half the Cree community of South Indian Lake, causing significant damage to fishing, hunting, and trapping in the region. In 1977 the Northern Flood Agreement established a process by which the Manitoba government would pay funds to people affected by this project.

April 12, 1974 ✦ Indian Financing Act
The U.S. Congress passed the Indian Financing Act, making available government funds to help finance "the economic development of Indians and Indian organizations."

June 17, 1974 ✦ *Morton* v. *Mancari*
The U.S. Supreme Court, in the case of *Morton* v. *Mancari,* upheld the preferential hiring of American Indians within the Bureau of Indian Affairs (BIA). The court pointed out that the government and the BIA had a special obligation to Indians.

June 17, 1974 ✦ Supreme Court upheld election
The U.S. Supreme Court refused to overturn a lower court decision upholding the election of an Arizona county supervisor who was a member of the Navajo

Comprehensive land claims in Canada.

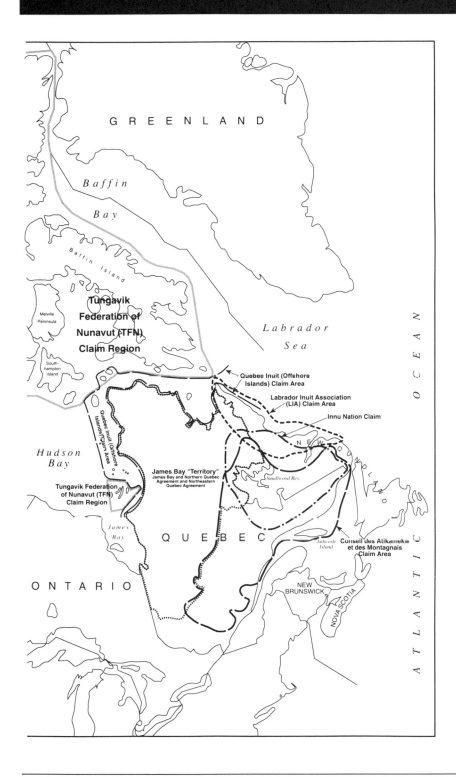

GREENLAND

Baffin

Bay

Baffin Island

Melville
Peninsula

**Tungavik
Federation of
Nunavut (TFN)
Claim Region**

South-
hampton
Island

*Labrador
Sea*

Quebec Inuit (Offshore
Islands) Claim Area

Labrador Inuit Association
(LIA) Claim Area

Innu Nation Claim

*Hudson
Bay*

Quebec Inuit (Offshore
Islands) Claim Area

**Tungavik Federation
of Nunavut (TFN)
Claim Region**

James Bay "Territory"
James Bay and Northern Quebec
Agreement and Northeastern
Quebec Agreement

N E W F O U N D L A N D

Smallwood Res.

*James
Bay*

Q U E B E C

*Anticosti
Island*

Conseil des Atikamekw
et des Montagnais
Claim Area

O N T A R I O

NEW
BRUNSWICK

NOVA SCOTIA

O C E A N

A T L A N T I C

nation. Non-Indian voters had challenged his eligibility for office on the grounds that his status as a reservation Indian made him immune from state taxes and the normal legal process.

September 15, 1974 ✦ "Native Caravan"

The "Native Caravan" began traveling from Vancouver, British Columbia, to Ottawa, Canada's capital. Indians in the caravan demanded settlement of their land claims and protested the poor housing conditions and social services on their reserves.

September 16, 1974 ✦ AIM leader released

Dennis Banks, American Indian Movement (AIM) cofounder, was freed following a six-month trial on charges arising from the 1973 riot over the mistreatment of a murder victim's mother by officials in Custer, South Dakota.

1975 ✦ Canadian land claims

Many of the lands and other benefits that were promised to Indians by treaty in Canada had not been delivered, leading several Indian nations to file land claims. Land claims in Canada fell into two groups—comprehensive and specific. Comprehensive land claims were made when an aboriginal (original inhabitants of the land) people could show that they had not given up their rights to the land. Aboriginal title to Native lands was supported by King George's Royal Proclamation of 1763. This decree stated that aboriginal people owned the land unless they had specifically given it up. In other words, they still owned any land they had not given up by signing a treaty. Many Native groups in Canada made comprehensive claims. *(See map, pages 140 and 141.)*

Specific claims involved disputes over particular promises given by treaty. These may have involved lands that were not given as promised, or resources such as cattle that were not provided. Some First Nations (Canada's Native peoples) claimed that Native lands and resources had been mismanaged, and therefore the government must repay the band for resulting losses. Numerous specific claims of this type were filed, and several were settled.

1975 ✦ Indian Self-Determination and Education Assistance Act

The Indian Self-Determination and Education Assistance Act was passed. This act gave tribal governments the power to arrange for services once provided by the Bureau of Indian Affairs. The legislation also provided federal funds to build needed public school facilities on or near Indian reservations.

January 8, 1975 ✦ Pine Ridge election ruled invalid

The 1974 election for the chairman of the Oglala Sioux Tribal Council, in which Richard Wilson defeated Russell Means (leader of AIM), was reviewed by the

U.S. Commission on Civil Rights. The commission found that the election was invalid, reporting that "almost one-third of all votes cast appear to have been in some manner improper," and that there had been almost no security measures to prevent fraud. The Justice Department, however, took no action on the commission's finding. Wilson's election and leadership prompted the uprising at Wounded Knee. Means, a traditionalist, had promised to destroy the "white man's tribal government" of the Oglala Sioux, while Wilson, an assimilationist (one who promotes the adoption of the dominant culture) had pledged full cooperation with the federal government. *(Also see entry dated February 27-May 8, 1973: Wounded Knee II.)*

March 14, 1975 ✦ American Indian Film Festival
The American Indian Film Festival opened in Seattle, Washington. The festival was dedicated to the presentation of American and Canadian Indians in the cinema. In 1978 the festival began an annual awards ceremony honoring its filmmakers and actors.

June 26, 1975 ✦ Federal Bureau of Investigation officers killed
Violence continued on the Pine Ridge Reservation after the Wounded Knee II takeover had ended. On June 26, 1975, two Federal Bureau of Investigation (FBI) officers were killed in a gun battle on the reservation. On November 25, 1975, a federal grand jury charged four Indians, Leonard Peltier, Robert Eugene Robideau, Darrelle Dean Butler, and James Theodore Eagle, on charges of murder. *(Also see entry dated April 16, 1977: Peltier found guilty.)*

July 19, 1975 ✦ Dene Declaration
The Indian Brotherhood of the Northwest Territories (Dene Nation) and the Métis Association of the Northwest Territories issued the "Dene Declaration" claiming that the aboriginal peoples of the Northwest Territories of Canada formed a nation with the right to self–government. ("Dene" means "people" in most Athapaskan dialects.) The Dene demands were rejected by the Canadian government in 1977.

August 6, 1975 ✦ Voting Rights Act Amendments of 1975
President Gerald Ford signed into law the Voting Rights Act Amendments of 1975. The act, which was designed to protect the voting rights of non-English speaking citizens by permitting voting in more than one language, specifically included American Indians.

November 11, 1975 ✦ James Bay and Northern Quebec Agreement
The Inuit of northern Quebec and the James Bay Cree were involved in the first modern land claims agreement to be reached in Canada. This agreement guaranteed hunting and fishing rights over parts of northern Quebec, and "own-

Creek actor Will Sampson starring with Jack Nicholson in the movie *One Flew over the Cuckoo's Nest.*

ership" of other parcels of land. It also established the Kativik regional government for the Inuit of the area, rights to education and use of the Inukitut language, and a cash and royalties settlement amounting to $90 million for the Inuit. In return, the Inuit and Cree gave up any claim to other lands.

February 1976 ✦ Oscar nomination

Will Sampson, a Creek actor, was nominated for the Academy Award for best supporting actor for his portrayal of Chief Bromden in the movie *One Flew over the Cuckoo's Nest* (1975). Sampson did not win the Oscar but went on to work in a number of films.

April 27, 1976 ✦ Taxes on reservations

The U.S. Supreme Court, in the case of *Moe* v. *Salish and Kootenai Tribes,* ruled that the states may not tax either personal property or cigarette sales by Indians to Indians on the reservation. The court ruled, however, that states could tax cigarette sales on reservations by Indians to non-Indians. This was a blow to tribal economic development.

Indian groups have fought until the present day to win the right to control taxation on reservations. Tribal governments have considered this power essential to their ability to be truly self-governing. Disputes over this issue have not yet been completely resolved.

May 1976 ✦ First Native college in Canada

The Saskatchewan Indian Federated College was organized as the first college in Canada under Native control.

May 29, 1976 ✦ Indian Crimes Act of 1976

The U.S. Congress passed the Indian Crimes Act of 1976. The act ensured that all individuals, Indian and non-Indian alike, would receive equitable treatment for crimes in all territories under federal supervision, including Indian reservations, military installations, and national parks.

September 16, 1976 ✦ Indian Health Care Improvement Act

The U.S. Congress passed the Indian Health Care Improvement Act. The bill provided increased funds for recruiting and training Indian health professionals; providing health services, including patient, dental, and alcoholism care; constructing and renovating health facilities; and providing services to urban Indians.

October 10, 1976 ✦ Native American Awareness Week

President Gerald Ford proclaimed the week of October 10 as Native American Awareness Week.

December 13, 1976 ✦ Navajo radio network

The Navajo radio network broadcast its first day of news and public interest programming on the reservation in the Navajo language.

April 15, 1977 ✦ Berger Inquiry

A pipeline was proposed to carry oil from Alaska southward through the Northwest Territory of Canada. The Berger Inquiry was set up to study this plan and reported that time was needed for Indians and the Inuit to settle their land claims with the government and for the residents to prepare for changes the development would bring. The report pointed out that residents feared the development and that Indians had not benefited from northern developments in the past. In 1980 the Dene and Métis of the Northwest Territories approved the pipeline.

April 16, 1977 ✦ Peltier found guilty

American Indian Movement leader Leonard Peltier was found guilty of two charges of first-degree murder in the shooting deaths of two Federal Bureau of Investigation (FBI) agents on the Pine Ridge Reservation in 1975. He was sentenced to, and is serving, two consecutive life terms. Peltier was the only one of the four men arrested in the shooting to be convicted of murder. In many foreign nations, and among many U.S. groups, Peltier has been considered a political prisoner of the United States. There have been frequent movements to free him. New evidence regarding the Pine Ridge shoot-out has been discovered, discrediting Peltier's involvement in the death of the FBI agents. *(Also see entry dated June 26, 1975: Federal Bureau of Investigation officers killed.)*

May 18, 1977 ✦ American Indian Policy Review Commission

The U.S. Congress released the American Indian Policy Review Commission Report. The study recommended that tribes be recognized as sovereign entities with the right to maintain their own judicial systems, to tax, and to control their own resources. The report also called for the abolition of the Bureau of Indian Affairs and the formation of a new agency that would better represent Native Americans and their interests.

June 13-17, 1977 ✦ Inuit Circumpolar Conference

Two hundred Native people from Alaska, Canada, and Greenland met for the first Inuit Circumpolar Conference. The conference was the first attempt to organize the 100,000 Inuit who inhabited the North Pole region. Delegates adopted resolutions concerning the preservation of their cultures, recognition of political rights to self-rule, environmental protection, and the banning of all weapons testing and disposal in the Arctic.

June 17, 1977 ◆ Indians and human rights

The International Indian Treaty Council, representing 97 tribes, provided the Soviet Union with a list of human rights abuses by the United States against Native American tribes. The list, which included treaty violations, the destruction of Native cultures and religions, and the interference in tribal economic and social life, would be used by the Soviets at the upcoming meetings on the Helsinki Accords. The Helsinki Accords, signed by 35 nations in 1975, pledged that each country would respect the self-determination and human rights of all peoples.

August 15, 1977 ◆ Native American Public Broadcasting Consortium

The Native American Public Broadcasting Consortium (NAPBC) was established. The NAPBC was an educational, nonprofit corporation offering the nation's largest high-quality library of Native American programs for public television and general use. By assisting Indian producers, the NAPBC worked to bring a new perspective to the national public television audience through American Indian programs.

September 1977 ◆ Alaskan Eskimo Whaling Commission

The Alaskan Eskimo Whaling Commission was founded to fight the International Whaling Commission's ban on the hunting of all bowhead whales. The Alaskan Eskimo Whaling Commission committed itself to ensure that all hunts were conducted in a traditional and nonwasteful manner, to educate non-Native Alaskans about the cultural importance of whaling, and to promote scientific research to ensure the bowhead whale would survive.

December 8, 1977 ◆ Indians and the Canadian legal system

The Native Council of Canada condemned the effects of the Canadian justice system on Natives. It claimed that the large number of Indians in jails were caused by high unemployment, little education, poverty, and lack of opportunities among Natives.

1978 ◆ Tribal colleges

The U.S. Congress passed legislation providing support for additional tribal colleges. Tribal colleges made special efforts to help Native American students achieve success. Because of the long history of academic failure on reservations, many students did not believe that they could succeed, or that college would be worthwhile. Some students carried generations of hostility toward schools.

Tribal colleges began by preparing Indian students to think of themselves as capable learners. Many Native students were older than the usual college age

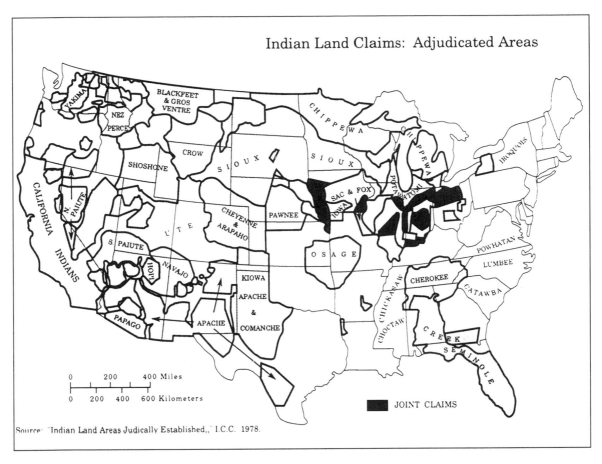

Indian Land Claims: Adjudicated Areas

0   200   400 Miles
0   200   400   600 Kilometers

■ JOINT CLAIMS

Source: "Indian Land Areas Judically Established," I.C.C. 1978.

A map showing U.S. Indian land claims established by court judgement, as published in the *Final Report,* Indian Claims Commission, 1978.

or were single parents returning to school after a long absence. Learning skills, personal speaking, social skills, and other classes developed self-confidence in these and other Native students.

The colleges also provided academic programs that prepared students to transfer to four-year colleges or universities. All tribal colleges included courses in Native languages and cultures, and most offered Native American Studies degrees.

Tribal colleges also worked with tribal elders and cultural leaders to write down and record traditional literatures and arts. Preserving cultural traditions was an important goal. Another goal was to extend these traditions out into the non-Indian community, by sponsoring traditional activities and tournaments.

Tribal colleges were successful. One survey found that students who attended tribal colleges immediately after finishing high school were eight times more likely to finish college than students who went to off-reservation colleges.

March 6, 1978 ✦ *Oliphant* v. *Suquamish Indian Tribe*

When two non-Indians were arrested by Suquamish tribal police for disturbing the peace and resisting arrest during the tribe's annual Chief Seattle Days, the non-Indian defendants brought the case to the Supreme Court. They argued that Indian tribes do not have the right to prosecute non-Indians.

The U.S. Supreme Court, in the case of *Oliphant* v. *Suquamish Indian Tribe,* agreed, ruling that non-Indians could not be tried in tribal courts for offenses committed on reservations. This was a major blow to tribal independence.

June 1978 ✦ Canadian constitutional reform

The Canadian federal government's discussion paper *A Time for Action* called for Native constitutional issues to be addressed and identified in the upcoming constitutional reform process. Constitutional reform became an important issue after Quebec elected a separatist government in 1976. Quebec, the only predominately French-speaking province in Canada, was threatening to secede from (leave) Canada. *(Also see entry dated February 5-6, 1979: Canadian constitutional talks begin.)*

June 8, 1978 ✦ Council of Energy Resource Tribes

Over 200 billion tons of coal, or 13 percent of the total U.S. reserves, was found on Indian reservations in the West. Reservation lands also accounted for about 4.2 billion barrels of oil and 17.5 trillion cubic feet of natural gas. Uranium was an important mineral resource on some reservations, particularly for the Navajo and Laguna Pueblo tribes.

These energy resources provided significant income for the 42 members of the Council of Energy Resource Tribes (CERT). CERT was formed by Indian tribes to negotiate and oversee the sale and use of oil, gas, coal, and minerals. Before the council was formed, BIA officials had frequently sold Indian resources at prices well below market value.

Although tribes received royalties from the sale of their resources, minerals have not always brought the prosperity they could to tribes. Many of the jobs in the oil and coal-mining industries required skills that people on reservations usually did not have. Also, many of the higher-paying jobs were given to union members rather than local workers.

July 1978 ✦ "The Longest Walk"

Several hundred Native Americans marched into Washington, D.C., at the end of "The Longest Walk." The Longest Walk was a protest that had started in San Francisco five months earlier. It was intended to symbolize the forced removal of Native Americans from their homelands over the past centuries and to draw attention to their continuing problems. The Longest Walk was a peaceful and

148

spiritual event that ended without violence. This was considered the last major event of the Red Power movement.

As the Red Power movement declined, the federal government reviewed its policies toward Indians in a new light. Government officials were well aware of Red Power actions and the changes in public opinion that resulted. The activism of the Red Power movement had a great impact on the condition of Native Americans in the United States.

August 13, 1978 ✦ American Indian Religious Freedom Act

President Jimmy Carter signed the American Indian Religious Freedom Act. The act was designed to "protect and preserve for American Indians their inherent right of freedom to believe, express and exercise their traditional religions." The legislation was intended to reverse a long history of governmental actions designed to destroy tribal religions.

September 5, 1978 ✦ Federal Acknowledgment Program

The Bureau of Indian Affairs (BIA) published regulations for the newly organized Federal Acknowledgement Program. This program was responsible for producing a set of "procedures for establishing that an American Indian group exists as an Indian tribe." Indians at first welcomed this program, but later discovered that the specific requirements involved in becoming recognized as a tribe were complicated and difficult for many Indian tribes to meet.

November 1978 ✦ First Indian-owned television station

The Oglala Sioux tribe announced plans to construct the first television station in the United States owned and operated by Native Americans. The station would serve the 14,000 people who lived on the Pine Ridge Reservation in South Dakota.

1979 ✦ Native Declaration of Rights

The Native Council of Canada issued its *Declaration of Métis and Indian Rights*. The document claimed Natives had rights to self–determination, to representation in legislatures and in the constitutional reform process, and to recognition of special status in the Canadian confederation.

February 5-6, 1979 ✦ Canadian constitutional talks began

Canada's first ministers (prime minister and premiers) met to discuss constitutional reform. Native groups complained because they were not allowed to participate in these meetings and wanted to be considered, along with persons of English and French descent, as a founding people of Canada. The first ministers decided on June 9, 1980, that Indian groups would be invited to participate only in discussions that directly affected them. *(Also see entry dated June 1978: Canadian constitutional reform.)*

Larry Pierre of the Okanagan, during the 1980 First Nations Constitutional Conference, demanding Native participation in constitutional tasks.

July 21, 1979 ◆ **Jay Silverheels' star**

Jay Silverheels, who played Tonto in the television series *The Lone Ranger,* was the first Indian actor to have a star placed on the Hollywood Walk of Fame. *(Also see entry dated March 1938:* The Lone Ranger *released.)*

October 31, 1979 ◆ **Archaeological Resources Protection Act of 1979**

The U.S. Congress passed the Archaeological Resources Protection Act of 1979 to protect all important archaeological sites on federal public lands and Indian lands.

1980s ◆ **Activism in the 1980s**

During the 1980s, Indian activism shifted its focus from public demonstration to court action. The number of Native American lawyers increased greatly, and Native Americans increasingly used the legal system to fight for their rights. Three main goals were targeted:

1) Land claims. Many tribes were fighting to have land they legally owned returned to them. Some of these claims were successful, some not.

2) The return of Indian artifacts (objects left behind by ancient civilizations, such as tools and ornaments). Many items stolen by explorers, settlers, and archaeologists were returned to Indian tribes.

3) The right of tribes to govern themselves. Many Native American tribes fought for control of water rights, hunting and fishing rights, and mineral and resource rights. They sought religious freedoms and the right to develop manufacturing, tourism, recreation, and other businesses on the reservations. Running gambling parlors on reservations was a controversial issue in many areas.

April 1980 ◆ **Indian health**

The Indian Health Service issued a report stating that tuberculosis and gastroenteritis were no longer the most important problems facing Indians. Indian health priorities now included "accidents, alcoholism, diabetes, mental health, suicides and homicides" caused by "changes in their traditional life-styles and values, and from depredation." ("Depredation" means to have had one's home and community savagely robbed and destroyed.)

April 13, 1980 ✦ Native American vice-presidential candidate
When the Citizen's Party selected environmentalist Barry Commoner as its nominee for president, LaDonna Harris, a Comanche Indian activist from Oklahoma, became his vice-presidential running mate.

April 15, 1980 ✦ Cherokee court defeat
The U.S. Court of Appeals dismissed a suit brought by members of the Eastern Cherokee who were seeking to prevent the construction of the Tellico Dam in eastern Tennessee. Tribal members argued that the dam, a project of the Tennessee Valley Authority, would flood ancestral lands sacred to the Cherokee and thus violate their First Amendment right to practice their religion freely. The court ruled that this land was not essential to the practice of the tribe's religion. The dam began flooding Cherokee land in November 1980.

June 14, 1980 ✦ Mohawk dispute
New York state sent 70 police to Akwesasne, the St. Regis Mohawk Indian reservation along the Canadian-U.S. border. The police served as a barrier between two armed and hostile groups on the reservation. The dispute between the two groups, which had lasted for more than 100 years, had grown to the point of civil war in the last year. The conflict was between traditionalists, who supported the leadership recognized in the past by the Iroquois confederacy, and those who supported the elected tribal government, which was favored by the federal and state governments.

June 22, 1980 ✦ Kateri Tekakwitha honored by Pope
The Vatican—the headquarters in Rome of the Catholic church—beatified Kateri Tekakwitha, a Mohawk-Algonquin Indian who had died 300 years previously at the age of 24. The beatification process is the last step before becoming a Catholic saint. She was the first American Indian to be beatified by the Catholic church.

June 24, 1980 ✦ Life on Canadian reserves
A Canadian federal report stated that alcoholism, unemployment, and poor living conditions were leading to family breakdown on Indian reserves.

June 30, 1980 ✦ *U.S.* v. *Sioux Nation.*
The U.S. Supreme Court in *U.S.* v. *Sioux Nation* upheld the $122 million judgment against the United States by the Court of Claims for the illegal taking of the Sioux Nation's Black Hills. The Sioux's treaty with the United States in 1868

had clearly guaranteed the Black Hills, or *Paha Sapa,* an area of sacred significance, to the tribe.

July 17, 1980 ◆ Female members of Parliament opposed Indian Act

Twenty-eight female members of the Canadian Parliament from all political parties announced that they would fight for the repeal of a section of the Indian Act that denied Indian status to Indian women (and their children) when they married non-Indians. *(Also see entry dated June 28, 1985: Indian Act amended.)*

December 2, 1980 ◆ Indians won human rights decision

The Russell Tribunal, an international human rights group located in the Netherlands, found the United States, Canada, and several countries in Latin America guilty of cultural and physical genocide (destruction) and of the unlawful seizure of land in their treatment of their Native populations. The decision had no legal authority.

January 30, 1981 ◆ Canadian government accepted Indian demands

The Canadian federal government accepted a constitutional amendment that would include the provisions of the Proclamation of 1763. (This proclamation stated that aboriginal people owned land unless they had specifically given it up.) Another amendment would read, "The aboriginal and treaty rights of the aboriginal peoples of Canada are hereby recognized and affirmed." *(Also see entries dated 1763: Proclamation of 1763; February 5-6, 1979: Canadian constitutional talks begin; and 1982: Constitution and Charter of Rights and Freedoms.)*

May 8, 1981 ◆ Tribal leaders opposed Watt

One hundred fifty tribal leaders, attending the National Tribal Government Conference in Washington, D.C., sent a letter to President Ronald Reagan demanding the immediate resignation of Secretary of Interior James G. Watt. The group claimed that Watt did not consult them as he was legally obligated to do. The tribal leaders also opposed Reagan's plans to reduce federal funds for adult and child education, housing, employment, assistance, and vocational training programs.

June 11, 1981 ◆ Indian civil rights

The U.S. Civil Rights Commission issued a major report on the federal government's treatment of American Indians. The commission, after a decade of research, proposed several changes in federal policy toward tribes. Among these changes was the establishment of an Office of Indian Rights within the Civil Rights Division of the Justice Department. The report also urged the government to work quickly to resolve fishing rights disputes and eastern land claims.

December 16, 1981 ✦ "In All Fairness"
John Munroe, Canadian minister of Indian Affairs, released "In All Fairness," a new Native claims policy, which accepted aboriginal land title in areas not covered by treaties and announced the government's intention to negotiate fair and equitable settlements that would allow Native people to live the way they wished. It also promised to speed up the land claims process.

1982 ✦ Constitution and Charter of Rights and Freedoms
Canada's new Constitution and Charter of Rights and Freedoms was proclaimed by the British government. Native Americans won a major battle when Canada constitutionally recognized aboriginal peoples. The Constitution officially divided Canada's aboriginal nations into three designations: the Indian, the Inuit, and the Métis peoples. Today these groups prefer to be known as "First Nations," since their ancestors were the first known inhabitants of present-day Canada.

Native groups were unhappy with two major parts of the new Constitution. First, they felt that their treaty rights were not adequately protected. Second, Indian groups argued that they should be given the right to self-government. First Nations organizations demanded a separate level of government to control Indian programs and land. This dispute led to years of negotiations and has still not been resolved. *(Also see entries dated March 26-27, 1987: Canadian constitutional conference; June 22, 1990: Meech Lake Accord defeated; August 20, 1992: Charlottetown Accord; and October 26, 1992: Charlottetown Accord defeated.)*

1982 ✦ Native-owned electric plant
The Warm Springs Indians of Oregon opened their own hydroelectric plant, the first Indian tribe to do so. This tribe also owned a logging operation, which included a sawmill and a plywood plant, and a resort and convention center.

January 7, 1982 ✦ Nuclear Waste Policy Act of 1982
The U.S. Congress passed the Nuclear Waste Policy Act of 1982. Several tribes opposed the bill because they were afraid it would lead to the destruction of Indian lands. The act called for the development of nuclear waste dump sites on Indian lands. *(Also see entry dated February 1-4, 1994: Apache signed nuclear waste storage agreement.)*

June 11, 1982 ✦ Tlingit sought apology
Tlingit Indians arrived in Washington, D.C., seeking an official apology from the U.S. Navy for its shelling of their village in the Admiralty Islands in 1882. The navy's actions were undertaken as a means of forcing the Alaskan Indians to return to work for private whalers.

August 14, 1982 ♦ Navajo Code Talkers Day

President Ronald Reagan declared August 14 as National Navajo Code Talkers Day, commemorating the group of Navajo servicemen who sent messages in their tribal language during World War II. The system was never cracked by the Germans or Japanese. *(Also see entry dated 1941-45: World War II and the Navajo Code Talkers.)*

1983 ♦ Indian Land Consolidation Act

The U.S. Congress passed the Indian Land Consolidation Act to help reduce the fragmentation of Indian lands. There were more than 54 million acres of Indian land. About 42 million acres of this land was owned by tribes, and about 11 million acres was owned, under Bureau of Indian Affairs control, by individuals. Most of these lands had been so split up by past government policies, they did not represent the same opportunities that they might otherwise. In addition, Native American lands could not be used as collateral to back up a loan. This made it very difficult for Indian landowners to get loans for farm equipment, seeds, and fertilizer.

1983 ♦ Métis National Council

The Métis National Council was founded. The council was made up of descendants of the Red River Métis who emerged in the late 1700s and early 1800s. The Métis (meaning "mixed") descended from unions between French or Scottish fur traders and aboriginal people.

January 24, 1983 ♦ Reagan's Indian policy

President Reagan issued the first Indian policy statement since 1975. Emphasizing that "the Constitution, treaties, laws, and court decisions have consistently recognized a unique political relationship between Indian tribes and the United States," the president stated his commitment to deal with Indian tribes on a "government-to-government" basis. Reagan claimed to want to encourage increased tribal self-sufficiency. "Tribal governments, like State and local governments, are more aware of the needs and desires of their citizens than is the Federal Government and should, therefore, have the primary responsibility for meeting those needs."

The address also promoted economic development on reservations and stated the government's support for industrial development of resources on Indian lands. Tribes and the American society "stand to gain from the prudent development and management of the vast coal, oil, gas, uranium, and other resources found on Indian lands." The address was met with skepticism by many Indian leaders, who were afraid that Reagan was considering a return to the policy of termination.

September 13, 1983 ✦ Dennis Banks surrendered

American Indian Movement cofounder Dennis Banks surrendered to state authorities in Rapid City, South Dakota, after nine years as a fugitive. Banks's surrender allowed the state to prosecute him for assaulting and rioting charges stemming from the 1973 Wounded Knee takeover and for flight to avoid prosecution. Banks, who stated that he feared for his life, explained that he had given himself up for the sake of his family. Banks had spent six years in California, under the protection of Governor Jerry Brown, before fleeing to the Onondaga Reservation in New York when Brown's successor, Governor George Deukmejian, indicated his willingness to extradite (return) Banks to South Dakota. New York governor Mario Cuomo had agreed to return Banks to South Dakota but had forbidden marshals to enter the Onondaga reservation near Syracuse, New York. On October 8, 1984, Banks was sentenced to three years in prison. On November 22, 1985, he was paroled. *(Also see entry dated February 27-May 8, 1973: Wounded Knee II.)*

Dennis Banks.

October 1, 1983 ✦ American Indian Registry for the Performing Arts

The American Indian Registry for the Performing Arts, an organization for Indians in the media, was established. The agency published an annual American Indian Talent Directory and worked as a liaison with studios, producers, and casting directors to promote the hiring of Native Americans within the motion picture industry.

November 3, 1983 ✦ Penner Report

The Penner Report, issued by a Canadian parliamentary committee, recommended that the aboriginal right to self-government should be included in the Constitution. The report suggested that Indian governments should be formed as a distinct level of government, with authority to control reserve land and resources.

1984 ✦ Education in Canada

The Canadian Education Association reported that Indian bands that had taken over control of Indian education had shown marked improvement in student achievement. Since 1970 increasing numbers of Indian bands had taken over control of Indian education.

INDIAN CULTURAL SURVIVAL SCHOOLS

In Canada, Indian Cultural Survival Schools were established. These schools devoted about half their time to teaching Indian culture. Indian materials were used for academic subjects when possible. Science courses often stressed ecology and the traditional Indian relationship between people and the environment.

Several schools featured a cultural survival camp, where staff and students went to a reserve for one week to live with elders in the traditional way. Elders taught students the traditional skills, told stories and legends, and performed rituals such as sweat lodge and pipe ceremonies. Students also learned traditional values such as sharing, cooperation, self-reliance, respect, and responsibility by participating in the day-to-day running of the camp. Some schools taught entirely in an Indian language, with English being introduced later.

March 25, 1984 • Cherokee united

Members of the Eastern Cherokee and the Cherokee Nation of Oklahoma held their first joint council meeting in 146 years. An estimated 10,000 tribal members attended the historic meeting held at the Cherokees' sacred ground in Red Clay, Tennessee. The two tribes, who confirmed their permanent split, agreed to meet annually in the Council of Cherokees to discuss issues and needs of common concern.

November 30, 1984 • Commission on Indian Reservation Economies

The Presidential Commission on Indian Reservation Economies presented its report to President Ronald Reagan. The report called for the abolition of the Bureau of Indian Affairs, claiming that most of its funds never reached Indian tribes, and recommended the reduction of the power of tribal governments over Indian businesses and societies. The National Tribal Council Association rejected the proposal, stating that it was against the "Indian way" of doing business, which was "to go into business to provide income for tribal members, to provide employment for as many tribal members as you can."

March 5, 1985 • Indian calendars

The *Journal of the Society for American Archaeology* reported that scientists, through the analysis of Winnebago calendar sticks, had the first evidence that ancient tribes, through systematic astronomical observations, had developed advanced full-year calendars.

May 7, 1985 • Canadian funding cuts recommended

The findings of the Nielson Task Force, created to find ways to reduce government spending, were leaked (given secretly) to the news media. The report urged the abolition of the Department of Indian Affairs and urged the government to stop negotiating comprehensive land claims. The report also said that to save money, the government should cut funding to Native housing, education, medical, economic, and land-claims programs. Indian organizations condemned the report, comparing it to the White Paper of 1969. Prime Minister Mulroney said the report was not government policy.

June 28, 1985 ✦ Indian Act amended

The Indian Act of 1876 in Canada was amended (changed). Women and their children who had lost their Indian status by marrying non-Indians were able to register as Indians once again. By 1991 about 92,000 Indians had registered to regain their status as Indians. *(Also see entry dated July 17, 1980: Female members of Parliament opposed Indian Act.)*

October 9, 1985 ✦ Canadian religious leaders backed Native rights

Leaders of the Roman Catholic, Anglican, Evangelical Lutheran, and United churches in Canada issued a call for the government to recognize aboriginal rights, including the right to self-government.

Indian chiefs open the first ministers' conference on aboriginal issues in Canada in March 1983. This was the first time aboriginals were given full participation at constitutional conferences.

Wilma Mankiller, principal chief of the Cherokee Nation.

December 1985 • *Living Treaties: Lasting Agreements*

Canadian Minister of Indian Affairs David Crombie issued *Living Treaties: Lasting Agreements* (the Coolican Report). This report announced a new government land claims policy, one which relied more on negotiation than on court cases. The policy also called for agreements that would allow Native peoples to share in the financial rewards of development in their territories. Native organizations welcomed the new policy as a breakthrough.

December 14, 1985 • Mankiller elected principal chief

Wilma Mankiller was sworn in as principal chief of the Cherokee Nation of Oklahoma. The nation, the largest Indian tribe in the country after the Navajo, was headed by a 15-member council. Mankiller became the first woman to lead a large tribe in modern history.

Under Mankiller the Cherokee sought to rebuild their communities. Both small and large community projects gave the Cherokee a renewed spirit. For example, men, women, and children laid 16 miles of pipe for running water in the tiny village of Bell. They also built a hydroelectric plant worth millions of dollars. Farming operations and defense plants were started. Mankiller said that the key to their success was that Cherokee never gave up.

1986 • Carolina Mirror Company

In an attempt to provide jobs for their children, the Eastern Cherokee bought the Carolina Mirror Company. Jobs would allow the Cherokee to support themselves in a non-Indian economy, while maintaining their self-reliance. Many Cherokee continued to live in poverty.

February 14, 1986 • Indian remains returned

The Smithsonian Institution's Museum of Natural History agreed to return Indian skeletal remains to tribal leaders for reburial, as required by spiritual belief. Studies had estimated that more than one million Indian remains were in the collections of museums and universities.

October 17, 1986 • Institute of American Indian and Alaska Native Culture and Arts Development

The Institute of American Indian and Alaska Native Culture and Arts Development was founded. The institute's goal was to acknowledge and promote the contributions of Native arts to American society.

The Mesquaki (Sauk and Fox) of Tama, Iowa, casino and bingo parlor, 1993.

October 27, 1986 ✦ Indian Alcohol and Substance Abuse Prevention and Treatment Act

Recognizing that alcoholism and other substance abuse were currently the most severe social and health problems facing Indian people, Congress passed the Indian Alcohol and Substance Abuse Prevention and Treatment Act. Native Americans were four times more likely to die from alcoholism than the general population. Four of the top ten causes of death among Indians were alcohol related.

November 1986 ✦ Indian Vietnam plaque dedicated

The Grandfather Plaque or Amerind Vietnam Plaque was dedicated at Arlington National Cemetery in Virginia. The plaque commemorated the service of approximately 43,000 indigenous combatants who served in the war in Vietnam. An estimated one out of every four eligible Indian males served in Vietnam.

November 6, 1986 ✦ Campbell elected to House of Representatives

Ben Nighthorse Campbell, a member of the Northern Cheyenne tribe of Montana, was elected to the U.S. House of Representatives from the third district of Colorado. Campbell was only the second Indian elected to the U.S. House of Representatives in recent times. Ben Reifel, a Sioux from South Dakota, served in the House from 1961 to 1971. *(Also see entry dated November 1992: Campbell elected to Senate.)*

March 26-27, 1987 ✦ Canadian Constitutional Conference

A Constitutional Conference on aboriginal issues ended with no agreement on how to define Indian rights to self-government and no agreement to meet again. Differences centered around the concept of the "inherent" aboriginal right to self-government. Aboriginal groups argued that their right to self-government was inherent—a right they had held since before Europeans came to North America and had never given up. Several provincial governments and the federal government were willing to recognize a government-granted and well-defined right to self-government. *(Also see entry dated 1982: Constitution and Charter of Rights and Freedoms.)*

September 18, 1987 ✦ Pope addressed Indian leaders

Pope John Paul II spoke to a group of 1,600 American Indian leaders in Phoenix, Arizona. The Pope urged the leaders to forget the past and to focus on the church's current support of Indian rights. In the past, the Catholic church had supported the Spanish colonists of the southwestern United States, whose treatment of Native groups had, at times, been quite brutal.

The Pope then traveled to Fort Simpson, Northwest Territories. He expressed sympathy with First Nations' desires for self-government and a hope that Canada would become a model in the way it treated Native peoples.

1988 ✦ Canadian Native Arts Foundation

The Canadian Native Arts Foundation (CNAF) was founded. The foundation was a privately and publicly funded national charity that provided scholarships for Native youths being trained in the arts. The CNAF was begun by John Kim Bell, a Mohawk symphony conductor and composer.

March 17, 1988 ✦ Indian suicide conference

The Warm Springs tribe of Oregon hosted a conference on suicide among Indians. The conference followed several suicides that had occured on the reservation inhabited by 2,800 members of the Wascoe, Paiute, and Warm Springs tribes. Six young people had killed themselves and 16 others had tried in the previous two months. Nationwide, young Indian men killed themselves at a rate more than twice the national average.

The conference, which was attended by Indian leaders and families as well as psychologists and social workers, sought in part to find the solution to the recent rise in suicide rates by returning to traditional practices and methods of counseling for young people.

October 17, 1988 ✦ Indian gambling

The Federal Indian Gambling Regulatory Act of 1988 allowed any tribe recognized by the U.S. government to engage in gambling activities. Reservation governments used the income from gambling to support their elderly and sick members and to pay for health care, housing, and other improvements. Some tribes have bought back ancient lands, restored sacred areas, worked to preserve traditional culture, established scholarship funds, and created jobs with income from the gambling industry. Although not all tribes agreed that gambling was a good type of development, to many tribes without other resources it was a necessary means to generate income.

November 1988 ◆ First Nations breakthroughs in Parliament

Wilton Littlechild, an Alberta Cree from the Progressive Conservative party, became the first treaty Indian elected to the House of Commons. Ethel Blondin, a Dene from Northwest Territories (Liberal party) became the first Native woman member of Parliament.

December 12, 1988 ◆ "Meeting Among Friends"

President Ronald Reagan held a meeting at the White House with 16 Indian leaders. Called the "Meeting Among Friends," it was the first meeting held at the White House between Indian leaders and the president of the United States in modern history. The meeting was planned after President Reagan made some offensive statements about Native Americans to students in the Soviet Union in May. One of Reagan's statements was: "Maybe we made a mistake. Maybe we should not have humored them [the Indians] in wanting to stay in that kind of primitive life style. Maybe we should have said: 'No come join us. Be citizens along with the rest of us.'" Reagan also said that many Indians had become very wealthy due to oil money. Indian leaders, pointing out that these statements were incorrect, raised questions about Reagan's lack of knowledge about the current state of Indian affairs.

1989 ◆ Indigenous Women's Network

The Indigenous Women's Network (IWN) was founded. Dedicated to meeting the needs of Native women, IWN sought to identify and communicate the issues and concerns of Native women. Specifically, IWN wished to focus on women working within their Native communities.

May 10, 1989 ◆ Great Whale Project

Cree of northern Quebec filed suit to stop construction of the Great Whale Project in northern Quebec. This hydroelectric development was the second part of the James Bay Project. The Cree were concerned that the Quebec government had begun construction without considering the impact this project would have on the environment. *(Also see entry dated September 10, 1991: Great Whale Project delayed.)*

June 24, 1989 ◆ Stanford University returned remains

Stanford University agreed to return and rebury the remains of 550 Ohlone Indians, the descendants of tribes in what is now the northern California area. Stanford was one of the first universities to agree to a repatriation (return) request by tribal leaders.

August 11, 1989 ◆ Centennial Accord

Governor Booth Gardner of Washington and the state's 26 federally recognized tribes signed the Centennial Accord. In the historic agreement, the state recog-

Many Native American leaders feel that urbanization could destroy their culture because many young Indians have never seen their reservations or spoken their Native language. The 1980 census showed that nearly 25 percent of Native Americans did not feel that they belonged to a tribe. Despite this, many urban Native Americans have tried to preserve their Native way of life and tribal leaders are still hopeful that Native American culture and traditions will survive.

January 26, 1990 ✦ Donald Marshall freed

An inquiry in Nova Scotia found that, because of racism and incompetence in the police force and legal community, Donald Marshall, a Micmac, had been wrongfully convicted of murder in 1972 and spent the next 11 years in prison. On February 7, 1990, the Nova Scotia government issued an apology to Marshall. The government announced that it would establish a cabinet committee on race relations and establish a Native criminal court as a test project.

February 27, 1990 ✦ Indian tribes united

Leaders of several North American tribes entered into an agreement to collectively (as a group) defend rights granted by their treaties with the government of the United States. Tribes from both the United States and Canada would assist each other with legal services and lobbying and law enforcement aid. The tribes also agreed to work together to educate the non-Indian public about federal treaties with Indians.

April 17, 1990 ✦ *Oregon* v. *Smith*

The U.S. Supreme Court ruled that a state ban on the use of peyote by American Indians did not violate the plaintiffs' First Amendment constitutional rights. The decision represented another blow to tribes in their efforts to protect their religious freedoms. *(Also see entry dated 1870-90: Peyote religion; and 1918: Native American church established.)*

June 22, 1990 ✦ Meech Lake Accord defeated

Indian organizations in Canada had opposed a constitutional reform package called the Meech Lake Accord because it did not include an amendment that would guarantee their right to self-government. Elijah Harper, an Ojibway-Cree member of the provincial legislature in Manitoba, was able to use parliamentary rules to prevent the passage of the Meech Lake Accord in the Manitoba legislature. Harper's maneuvers killed the accord because it was not passed in time by all Canadian provincial legislatures. Indians claimed this as a major victory and hoped the defeat of the Meech Lake Accord would force the government to negotiate on Indian self-government. *(Also see entry dated March 26-27, 1987: Canadian Constitutional Conference.)*

A Mohawk warrior and a Canadian soldier engage in a staring match during the 78-day standoff at Kanesatake (Oka), near Montreal.

July 2-3, 1990 ✦ Self-Governance Pilot Program
Assistant Secretary of the Interior Eddie Brown signed historic agreements with six tribes. These tribes were part of a Self-Governance Pilot Program that would ultimately allow up to 20 tribes the authority to administer and set priorities for federal funds received directly from the government.

July 11, 1990 ✦ Mohawk blockade
A police officer was killed after Quebec police stormed a barricade on the Mohawk reserve at Kanesatake (Oka), near Montreal. The Mohawk set up the blockade in March to prevent construction of a golf course on land they claimed. In sympathy with the Mohawk at Kanesatake, members of the Mohawk Warriors Society at Kahnawake, south of Montreal, blocked access to the Mercier Bridge, a bridge linking the southern suburbs of Montreal with the city. The

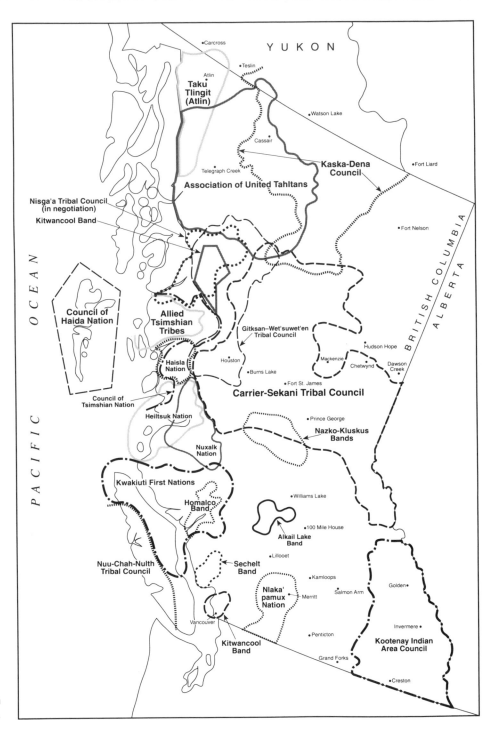

Land claims in
British Columbia.

actions began a 78-day standoff between the police and military and the Mohawk Warriors of Kahnawake and Kanesatake, a conflict that drew worldwide attention. *(Also see entry dated September 26, 1990: Mohawk standoff ended.)*

August 1990 ✦ Desmond Tutu visited Canada
South African Anglican Archbishop Desmond Tutu visited the Osnaburgh Ojibway Reserve in northwestern Ontario. He said that Canada's treatment of its Native people was similar in many ways to South Africa's treatment of blacks under the system of apartheid (the policy of segregating people by race).

August 3, 1990 ✦ American Indian Heritage Month
The U.S. Congress declared November as "American Indian Heritage Month."

August 9, 1990 ✦ British Columbia Indian policy
The British Columbia government announced that it was willing to join First Nations and the federal government in land claims negotiations assuming the legitimacy of aboriginal title. British Columbia had refused to negotiate with Native peoples about land claims since it joined Canada in 1864. *(Also see map on page 166.)*

September 25, 1990 ✦ Canadian Indian policy
Prime Minister Brian Mulroney announced a new government agenda to meet Indian grievances. He committed the government to speeding up settlement of all land claims and meeting all its outstanding treaty obligations. Mulroney also announced plans to improve housing, sewage treatment, and water facilities on reserves and to increase Indian control over their own affairs.

September 26, 1990 ✦ Mohawk standoff ended
The Mohawk warriors at Kahnawake and Kanesatake surrendered after an 11-week standoff with police and soldiers. The standoff attracted international attention and made Canadians more aware of the depth of frustration among many Native Canadians. The federal government had refused to negotiate with the Mohawks as long as the standoff continued. *(Also see entry dated June 11, 1990: Mohawk blockade.)*

October 4, 1990 ✦ Indian Environmental Regulatory Act
The U.S. Congress passed the Indian Environmental Regulatory Act. The act served to reinforce and clarify the authority of the federal government to protect areas of environmental concern in Indian Country.

One result of government control of Indian lands had been serious environmental problems. People who leased Indian land often left behind polluted water and soil. Leaking pesticide containers and underground storage tanks for gas had been common. Waste disposal systems on the reservations did not meet federal standards and were a major source of pollution and related health problems. The government did not deal with these problems, and the tribes did not usually have enough money to do so.

October 30, 1990 ◆ Native American Languages Act

The Native American Languages Act was passed by the U.S. Congress. The act was designed to preserve, protect, and promote the practice and development of Indian languages. This legislation was important since the federal government in the past had tried to destroy Indian languages. It is estimated that more than half of all Indian languages are now extinct. Approximately 250 Indian languages remain in existence, although some are spoken by only a few individuals.

Most of the aboriginal languages of Canada had been at risk of being lost for many years. Only three—Cree, Ojibway, and Inukitut—are spoken over large areas today. In light of this, many aboriginal communities tried to preserve Native languages by having language and culture programs in their schools.

November 16, 1990 ◆ Graves Protection and Repatriation Act

Acknowledging the wishes of individual tribes and national and local Indian organizations, the U.S. Congress passed the Native American Graves Protection and Repatriation Act. The act provided for the protection of American Indian grave sites and the repatriation (return) of Indian remains and cultural artifacts to tribes.

November 28, 1990 ◆ Indian Child Protection and Family Abuse Prevention Act

The Indian Child Protection and Family Abuse Prevention Act required tribes to report abusive situations and to establish tribal programs to treat and prevent future abuse. Historically a rare problem, child abuse was being experienced increasingly on tribal reservations.

November 29, 1990 ◆ Indian Arts and Crafts Act

The Indian Arts and Crafts Act was established to prevent the manufacture and sale of counterfeit Indian arts and crafts. With the increase in value of tribal artwork and jewelry, tribal artists had faced competition from non-Indian, machine-manufactured artworks.

December 29, 1990 ◆ Centennial of Wounded Knee massacre

Approximately four hundred people attended the centennial of the Wounded Knee massacre. On October 19 the U.S. House of Representatives provided the final approval needed for a resolution expressing "deep regret" over the Seventh Cavalry's massacre on the Pine Ridge reservation. *(Also see entry dated 1890: Ghost Dance and Wounded Knee.)*

168

1991-1992 ◆ Nunavut territory in Canada

For many years the Inuit in the Northwest Territories sought to establish a self-governing homeland to be known as "Nunavut," meaning "Our Land" in Inuk-itut. In a 1991 land settlement, the creation of a this new territory was proposed. It involved 350,000 square kilometers (135,000 square miles) of land and payment to the Inuit of $580 million. In return the Inuit gave up all rights to the rest of their traditional lands. As proposed, Nunavut would have the status of a province, and would also have an Inuit majority. In 1992 the residents of the Northwest Territories approved the boundary of Nunavut. The territory will be established by 1999.

April 1991 ◆ *Dances with Wolves*

Kevin Costner's *Dances with Wolves* (1990) sparked renewed interest in movies with Indian themes. This popular movie, which won seven Academy Awards including best picture of the year, cast many Indian actors and portrayed Indians sympathetically. Also, authentic Native languages were used. However, many observers felt that *Dances with Wolves* projected romanticized images of the "noble savage" and did not effectively change Hollywood's stereotyping of Indian life and people.

April 4, 1991 ◆ Census Bureau report on Indian population

The Census Bureau announced that 1,959,234 American Indians and Alaska Natives lived in the United States. Of these numbers, 1,878,285 were American Indian, 57,152 were Eskimo, and 23,797 were Aleut.

June 6, 1991 ◆ All-Native film studio created

The National Film Board of Canada announced the creation of Studio One, an all-Native studio. Studio One's purpose was to counter the misrepresentation of Canada's aboriginal people in mainstream media by providing production facilities and training for independent Indian filmmakers.

June 14, 1991 ◆ President Bush's Indian policy

President George Bush issued his policy statement on American Indians in which he reaffirmed his commitment to government-to-government relationship between the federal government and the Indian nations.

June 26, 1991 ◆ Abuses in Canadian education

The Canadian government announced that it would fund programs to help victims deal with lasting problems caused by abuse at government-run residential schools. Evidence of physical and sexual abuse at residential schools had been revealed in the past few years. Native leaders said that high rates of family breakdown, physical and sexual abuse, depression, alcoholism, and suicide were related to damage done by residential schools.

July 5, 1991 ✦ Native constitutional hearings

The Assembly of First Nations agreed to hold hearings to determine what kind of constitutional reforms Indians would support. The Assembly of First Nations (formerly the National Indian Brotherhood) represented status Indians (members of the 633 Canadian Indian bands registered with the government) in Canada.

September 7, 1991 ✦ Aboriginal law in Canada

Canadian federal justice minister Kim Campbell announced that she was willing to consider fundamental changes in Canada's justice system in an effort to solve the problems faced by aboriginal peoples. Campbell, however, rejected the concept of a separate Native justice system. The comment followed several provincial and federal reports calling for a separate Native justice system.

September 10, 1991 ✦ Great Whale Project delayed

A federal court judge ordered the Canadian government to delay the hydroelectric project known as the Great Whale Project until a strict environmental review had been carried out. The Cree had filed suit more than two years prior to the ruling to stop the Great Whale Project because of the severe repercussions it might have on the environment. *(Also see entry dated May 10, 1989: Great Whale Project.)*

September 18, 1991 ✦ Indian seats in House of Commons

The Canadian Royal Commission on Electoral Reform recommended that a number of seats in the House of Commons be set aside for aboriginal peoples to ensure that Native Canadians were adequately represented. Because Natives were a minority in almost every electoral district in the country, most were unable to elect Native politicians.

October 1991 ✦ Protests over "Tomahawk Chop"

Protests occurred before World Series games in Atlanta, Georgia, and Minneapolis, Minnesota, over the use by Atlanta Braves baseball fans of the cheer known as the "Tomahawk Chop." Native Americans claimed the cheer and the name "Braves" were disrespectful to Indians.

During the late 1980s and the early 1990s Native American groups were successful in having the Indian nicknames of many college athletic teams changed. Efforts continue to the present time to have several professional teams change their nicknames. These efforts have so far been unsuccessful.

October 28, 1991 ✦ Criminal Jurisdiction Act

Congress passed the Criminal Jurisdiction Act. The act established that Indian tribes had the power to exercise criminal jurisdiction over (to arrest and prosecute for crimes) Indian people on Indian reservations. Indian groups had fought

for many years to be able to arrest and try in tribal court all Indians and non-Indians who committed crimes on reservations. Several court cases had denied Indians the right to try non-Indians, making it difficult for tribal governments to control their reservations.

November 26, 1991 ◆ Custer Battlefield renamed

After considerable debate, the U.S. Congress renamed the Custer Battlefield

Nunavut, a stone lithograph by Inuit artist Kenojuak Ashevak, commemorating the Nunavut claim in the eastern Arctic.

National Monument in eastern Montana as the Little Bighorn Battlefield Monument. Indian groups had asked for the change.

August 17, 1992 ✦ Native church leader

Stanley J. McKay, a Cree from Beausejour, Manitoba, was elected moderator (national leader) of the United Church of Canada, the country's largest Protestant church denomination.

August 20, 1992 ✦ Charlottetown Accord

Canadian Prime Minister Brian Mulroney, Canada's ten premiers, and the leaders of the Assembly of First Nations and other Native organizations reached agreement on provisions that would include aboriginal self-government in Canada's Constitution (the Charlottetown Accord). On September 3 Prime Minister Mulroney announced that a national referendum (vote) on the Charlottetown Accord would be held October 26, 1992. *(Also see entries dated 1982: Constitution and Charter of Rights and Freedoms; June 22, 1990: Meech Lake Accord defeated; and October 26, 1992: Charlottetown Accord defeated.)*

October 26, 1992 ✦ Charlottetown Accord defeated

In a national referendum (vote), Canadians rejected the Charlottetown Accord. Included in the proposal for a new Constitution were sections that would grant aboriginals a form of self-government. Pollsters suggested that most Canadians did not reject the proposal because of its provisions about aboriginal self-government, although status Indians did not appear to support the proposal. Sixty-two percent of those on Indian reserves who voted rejected the accord. Many Natives complained that the self-government provisions were not adequately spelled out. Native leaders announced that they would use general public support for the idea of aboriginal self-government and continue their struggle through other means. *(Also see entry dated August 20, 1992: Charlottetown Accord.)*

November 1992 ✦ Campbell elected to Senate

Coloradans elected Ben Nighthorse Campbell to the U.S. Senate, the second Native American to serve there. Campbell had served in the U.S. House of Representatives since 1987. *(Also see entry dated November 6, 1986: Campbell elected to House of Representatives.)*

February 6, 1993 ✦ First annual Totem Awards

The First Annual Totem Awards were presented to outstanding Native American artists in film, television, theater, and music. The event was organized by First Americans in the Arts, an organization dedicated to encouraging the participation of Native Americans in the entertainment industry.

March 5, 1993 ◆ **First Métis lieutenant-governor**
Yvon Dumont was sworn in as the first Métis lieutenant-governor in Canada.

March 29, 1993 ◆ **Canadian national Native newspaper**
Windspeaker, published in Edmonton, Alberta, became the first national Native newspaper in Canada.

June-July 1993 ◆ **Navajo illness**
The hantavirus, a rodent-carried disease, was responsible for the deaths of 16 Indian people, primarily Navajo, in the Four Corners region of the southwestern United States. Initially specialists from the Indian Health Service in Albuquerque, New Mexico, stated, "We don't know what causes it," but guided in part by Navajo medicine men, researchers soon traced the disease to a growing population of rodents. While the majority of deaths had been Navajo, Indians of other tribes, and non-Indians as well, had contracted the fatal disease.

June 1, 1993 ◆ **Canadian census**
According to a Canadian census, 783,980 people in Canada identified themselves as Indian (626,000 were status Indians); 212,650 as Métis; and 49,255 as Inuit. Sixty-five percent of Canadian Natives lived west of Ontario.

July 1993 ◆ **First female assistant secretary of Indian affairs**
Ada Elizabeth Deer (Menominee) became assistant secretary of Indian affairs in the U.S. Department of the Interior. She was the first woman—and the sixth Indian—to fill the post.

November 1993 ◆ **Memorial honored Ute warriors**
About 1,000 people in Meeker, Colorado, gathered to honor the Ute warriors who died at the battle of Milk Creek in 1879. This was the nation's first memorial dedicated to Native American warriors and erected by Native Americans.

January 18, 1994 ◆ **Native self-government in Canada**
The Canadian government announced that it would work with Natives to implement aboriginal self-government. It also announced that it would speed up the land claims process, increase funding for aboriginal postsecondary education, and introduce an aboriginal head-start educational program.

February 1–4, 1994 ◆ **Apache signed nuclear waste agreement**
Apache leaders signed an agreement with Northern States Power, a Minnesota utility, to negotiate the construction of a private nuclear waste storage facility on their reservation in south-central New Mexico. The tribe felt that the economic benefit of the waste dump would outweigh the possible health effects the

facility would have on the people of the area. *(Also see entry dated January 7, 1982: Nuclear Waste Policy Act of 1982.)*

February 11–July 15, 1994 ✦ Walk For Justice 1994

American Indian Movement cofounders Dennis Banks and Mary Jane Wilson–Medrano led a "Walk for Justice" from Alcatraz Island in California to Washington, D.C., drawing public attention to Native issues and collecting signatures requesting the release of Leonard Peltier, who had served 18 years in prison for allegedly shooting two Federal Bureau of Investigation (FBI) agents on the Pine Ridge Reservation in South Dakota in 1975. *(Also see entries dated June 26, 1975: Federal Bureau of Investigation officers killed; and April 16, 1977: Peltier found guilty.)*

March 1994 ✦ Native American-African American alliance

The National Congress of American Indians, a confederation of 162 tribal governments and the nation's oldest and largest Indian organization, agreed to support the Black Caucus of State Legislators, a caucus of 540 African American state legislators from 42 states, in their struggles for African American rights. In December 1993, the Black Caucus of State Legislators passed a similar resolution to support Native American tribal sovereignty. Both groups agreed that since they shared similar histories of economic and political oppression in the United States, they needed to build coalition networks to fight for basic economic and human rights.

March 9, 1994 ✦ Geronimo Scholarship

Columbia Pictures and Sony Pictures Entertainment sponsored a scholarship program in connection with the release of the film *Geronimo: An American Legend.*

March 16-18, 1994 ✦ Indian Country Tourism 200 Conference

A national policy planning conference took place and addressed the issues and problems of developing a tourist market in American Indian communities.

INDEX

FEB   2001